A Memoir of the Rev. James Crabb ..

John Rudall

BIBLIOLIFE

A MEMOIR

OF THE

REV. JAMES CRABB,

LATE OF SOUTHAMPTON.

BY

JOHN RUDALL,

OF LINCOLN'S INN, BARRISTER-AT-LAW.

"He looked for a city which hath foundations, whose Builder and Maker is God."

LONDON:

WALTON AND MABERLY,

UPPER GOWER-STREET, AND IVY-LANE, PATERNOSTER-ROW.

MDCCCLIV.

LONDON
PRINTED BY WILLIAM TYLER,
BOLT-COURT.

PREFACE.

The materials from which the following Memoir has been framed consist of,—1st, three Diaries kept by Mr. Crabb—one commencing in the month of February, 1791, when he joined the Wesleyan Methodists, and terminating in the month of January, 1793; another commencing in the month of January, 1795, when he became an itinerant preacher, and ending in the month of December, 1798; and the other commencing in the year 1818, when he was resident at Rumsey, and which, with some intermissions, was continued down to the year 1825: 2ndly, a large collection of his letters: and 3rdly, a rough sketch of his life, which he drew up during his last illness, but which contains little additional information to that which his Diaries furnish.

These papers were, in the early part of last year, placed in my hands, with a request that as I had enjoyed the privilege of a long acquaintance with Mr. Crabb, and knew something of the labours in which he had spent his days, I would draw up a Memoir of his Life; and with this request, after much hesitation, I have in the following pages endeavoured to comply.

It would have been no difficult task to have extended
the Memoir to a much greater length, but as it was desirable to keep it in an inexpensive compass, brevity has
been studiously kept in view, though, probably, I may
have erred by too great a condensation.

The Memoir has been written with many inter-
ruptions, in intervals snatched from professional labours;
and this must be my excuse for the delay in the
publication, and the imperfections — which I fear are
many—with which it abounds. Christian reader, deal
forgivingly with these imperfections. My prayer for
thee is, that whatever there is of God's truth in these
pages may profit thy soul, serve to make Jesus more
precious to thee, stir thee up in these "perilous times"
to promote with more diligence His kingdom in this
world, and lead thee to higher communion with heaven.

16, WESTBOURNE TERRACE, HYDE PARK,
    December, 1853.

CONTENTS.

CHAPTER I.

CHAPTER II.

CHAPTER III.

CHAPTER IV.

CHAPTER V.

CHAPTER XV.

CHAPTER XVI.

CHAPTER XVII.

REV. JAMES CRABB.

CHAPTER I.

Introduction.—Birth and parentage.—Early religious impressions.
—His discouragements.—School-days.—Apprenticeship.—His
companions.—His conversion.—Attends Wesleyan ministry.—
His spiritual joy.—Joins the Wesleyans. -His devotedness and
piety.—Keeps a Diary.

It is the remark of Dr. Manton, that man is a ductile
creature, more apt to be led by the eye than the ear; and
this has ·been the experience of all ages. Hence the
advantage which example has over precept; for whilst the
latter appeals to the understanding, the former strikes the
eye and affects the heart. " Quemadmodum pictores,"
observes a wise heathen, " cum imaginem pingunt, identi-
dem exemplaria spectant: ita qui se studet omnibus
virtutis partibus perfectum efficere, debet ad mores et
vitas bonorum sæpe oculos convertere;"—(as painters, when
engaged in their art, make use of models to assist them;
so he who would attain to moral perfection should often
study the lives of good men;)—a piece of advice no less
useful to the man of God than to the mere moralist.
Our Lord, it is true, is the great Exemplar of his Church,
yet, as Jeremy Taylor has well observed, " He did many
things which his people are not to imitate, and they are

B

to do some things which they cannot learn from His example;" a truth fully borne out by the lives of holy men, recorded not only in the Scriptures, but by uninspired penmen; for in them were exhibited the conflicts between spirit and flesh — the reign of grace over inbred corruption—the triumphs of faith over unbelief, and those developments of Christian life and practice which were not, and could not, be exhibited by Him who possessed a sinless nature, and in whom Satan " had nothing." Hence it is that we are exhorted to be "followers of them who, through faith and patience, inherit the promises." Hence, also, the value of Christian biography. How many have been stirred up to acts of benevolence by the example of a Howard, excited to missionary zeal by the labours of a Schwartz, or a Henry Martin, or have given themselves (as he who is the subject of the following memoir did) to the work of saving souls, by the example of such men as Whitefield and Wesley, or been provoked unto love and good works by what has been recorded of a Wilberforce, a Buxton, or a Fry. " The very remembrance of good men," says Farindon, "is a degree and an approach unto holiness; and God has ordained that one Christian should be a lesson to another, which he should learn, and teach again, and strive to improve."

It is from these considerations, and in the hope that He " who inhabiteth the praises of Israel," may be glorified, that the following Memoir has been penned, in which are exhibited the labours, the Christian character, and experience of James Crabb, who, though but a little luminary in the Church's horizon, was, in the place he occupied, a bright and shining light, by which many were directed heavenwards, to the glory of Him from whom that light was derived.

This eminent servant of God was born at Wilton, in the county of Wilts, on the 13th of April, 1774. He was the third son of James Crabb, who carried on an extensive business as a clothier in that town. In his childhood he exhibited many indications of those peculiarities of character for which he was remarkable in after life. He was naturally of an ardent turn of mind, and was endued with an indomitable spirit, and that indispensable element of all greatness,—decision of character. At an early age his heart was deeply impressed with the solemn realities of eternity; he had an extraordinary reverence for the ministers of Christ, and his mind was so much drawn towards the sacred employment of the ministry that in the hours allotted to recreation he was accustomed to assemble his playmates in a wood belonging to his father, where, personating the minister, he addressed them, from a hollow tree which he used as a pulpit, upon their duties and conduct. At the age of ten years his serious impressions were deepened under the ministry of a Mr. Hook, of Wilton, by whom he was instructed in the Catechism; and so great was the esteem in which he held him, that when he removed from the town, James Crabb was, to use his own words, almost heartbroken. The religious impressions thus made upon his heart attracted the notice of his father, who, though well disposed towards religion, had so great a horror of what he termed Methodism, that he used every influence in his power to check the growing piety of his son, and, with this view, took occasion upon every act of disobedience which he committed, to declaim against his religious profession, and charge him with hypocrisy. But how unsearchable are the ways of God! In the appointed time the persecuting father was, through the instrumentality of that persecuted son,

to receive " an inheritance among them which are sanctified."

Young Crabb thus circumstanced, — having none to
counsel him, and meeting with no sympathy, but rather
discouragement at home,—associated with youths who,
like himself, were under no restraint, and by whom he
was soon corrupted. Having forgotten the instructions
he received from Mr. Hook, he went on "frowardly in the
way of his heart," and " departed from the living God."
In this backsliding state he was placed by his father at a
boarding-school in Shenfield; the proprietor of which, like
most of the schoolmasters of those days, was wholly unfit
to train or instruct the young. There he learnt nothing
more than the common rudiments of an English education : he received no religious instruction, nor had he
any advantage of moral training. It is no wonder therefore that bad habits were acquired, and the natural
corruptions of his heart strengthened; but God, who
watched over him with a Father's care, still dealt with his
conscience, and brought to his remembrance the lessons
of his earlier days, in the retrospect of which he often
wept, and in secret prayed.

At the end of two years he left school; and being
now in his fourteenth year, his father, without consult-
ing his taste, or ascertaining his capacity, apprenticed
him to a man, a professed Socinian, who carried on
a large shoemaking business in Salisbury. In this
business young Crabb was associated with three young
men,—of whom one was an infidel, another a backslider, and the other a young man of some piety, who
had connected himself with the Wesleyan Methodists,
and was striving, in spite of the discouragements by
which he was surrounded, to walk with God. The

influences to which young Crabb was now exposed pre-
ponderated on the side of evil; and being no longer under
parental restraint, he gave way to his corruptions—walked,
as he has himself recorded, "in the counsel of the
ungodly," and was well nigh sitting "in the seat of the
scornful;" but he was permitted for a while thus to walk,
that he might learn that most difficult of all lessons
to be acquired, " The heart of man is deceitful above all
things, and desperately wicked." At length the time
of his deliverance,—when he was to escape "as a bird
out of the snare of the fowler," arrived; and it was no
less sudden than striking. One night, in the month of
November, 1790, after he had retired to bed, a thunder-
storm, more violent than had ever been witnessed by the
oldest inhabitant of the place, passed over the city of
Salisbury. So awful was the fury of the elements that
the affrighted inhabitants rushed from their beds,
imagining that the judgments of God were coming upon
the earth. Amongst these was James Crabb, who,
filled with terror and dismay, and believing that the
vengeance of Heaven was about to overtake him for his
sins, fell down in deep abasement before Him whose
Spirit he had grieved, and in bitterness of soul cried for
that mercy which none ever sought, or shall seek, in vain.
From this moment he gave up his ungodly companions,
made an open profession of religion, and willingly bore
the ridicule to which his change of conduct exposed him.
Thus, under God,

> One thought
> Settles a life, an immortality!

He now began to feel that he could no longer attend the
heartless, Christless, services of the Socinian chapel, in
which he found nothing to satisfy the cravings of his

renewed heart; and therefore committing himself to the direction of Heaven by earnest prayer, he wrote an affectionate and dutiful letter to his father, entreating him to intercede with his master for permission to attend the Wesleyan chapel. "Call upon me in the day of trouble; I will deliver thee, and thou shalt glorify me," is the gracious promise of a faithful God, and his faithfulness was proved in this matter; for old Mr. Crabb, though he despised the Methodists, complied with his son's request; and the master, without demur, gave his assent.

And now began a new era in the life of James Crabb. His attendance at a Wesleyan place of worship led him into a clearer discovery of Gospel truth—he saw and felt his lost condition as a sinner—and fled for refuge to Him who came to seek and to save the lost. That he at this time passed through that great change which all, however amiable or moral, learned or refined, must undergo before they can see the kingdom of God here, or enter into it hereafter, and which is truly called a "turning from darkness to light, and from the power of Satan unto God," there can be no doubt; and he ever looked back upon this period of his life with satisfaction and thankfulness. He has recorded, that so greatly did he realise the change wrought in his soul, that he might have been seen running and leaping through the streets of Salisbury in ecstasies of joy;—and who that has been the subject of this great and glorious transition, has not felt in some degree the same, and entered in some measure into the experience of what is written, "Ye shall go out with joy, and be led forth with peace; the mountains and the hills shall break forth before you with singing, and all the trees of the field shall clap their hands?" On one particular day he was so overcome that he suddenly stopped in the street, and asked aloud, "What is it that makes me so happy?" when the words, "thy sins are forgiven thee," seemed to sound in his ears as though audibly addressed to him, and so impressed was he with the occurrence that he received it as, and ever believed it to have been, a Divine intimation to his soul that he was a pardoned sinner—an accepted child. This, however, was but the "beginning of days," the infancy of spiritual life. As the Israelites of old knew nothing of the great and terrible wilderness through which they had to pass, "wherein were fiery serpents, and scorpions, and drought," but imagined that on passing out of Egypt they should peaceably reach the promised land; so our young convert, knowing nothing of the life of faith, or of the difficulties and discouragements of the way, thought all was now accomplished, that his path would be strewed with never-fading flowers and lighted with perpetual sunshine: but he soon learnt that the pathway to heaven is one of much tribulation—that there is a cross to be borne, a warfare to be accomplished; and no man ever learnt those lessons more thoroughly than he afterwards did.

On the 28th of January, 1791, young Crabb, being then of the age of seventeen, was admitted a member of the Wesleyan body—a sect at that time despised, and "everywhere spoken against." He had, however, counted the cost, and he joined them with a full determination of making a total surrender of himself to God. He has recorded that at this time his great delight was prayer, and in this holy exercise he engaged seven stated times every day, to which he added frequent ejaculatory and mental prayer. Having connected himself with several God-fearing youths, he accompanied them to the early

prayer-meetings, which in those days were held before the
business of the day commenced. In order to secure their
early rising, he volunteered to call them at five o'clock in
the summer, and six in the winter; and being, as he has
recorded, a heavy sleeper, he used to tie a string to his
wrist, which he fastened to a wire communicating with the
street-door, that the watchman, to whom he paid a small
gratuity, might call him. Finding this method expensive,
he adopted the plan of sometimes lying down upon a stick
full of knots, on which he considered it unlikely he should
lie too long; at other times he tied a weight to one of his
feet, and let it swing at the foot of the bed, so that he was
sure to awake by the pulsation which the weight occasioned.

At this period of his life he began to keep a diary
in which he recorded the varying state of his heart,
the ebbings and flowings of Divine grace in his soul, and
his advances and retrogressions in the spiritual life—in
other words, a history of his Christian experience. A few
extracts from this record may serve to show the reality of
the work which was going on within him—the struggles of
a renewed heart against natural corruption—and the true
secret of progression in the Divine life.

CHAPTER II.

ON Thursday the 15th of February, 1791, being less than a month after he had joined the Wesleyans, he thus writes :

" In the morning, when I awoke, I found my mind in a good frame, but the Lord did not break in upon me with his presence till after prayer. In the afternoon, about one o'clock, I found my carnal nature stirring , Satan tempted me against striving after holiness of life—setting before me this person and that person who were not holy, though they had been in the way longer than I had ; but I did not mind him, and was troubled to think that I had, during the day, been overcome by anger,—I had, however, the wounds of Jesus to which I could fly. In the afternoon I did not seem to be breathing after sanctification as earnestly as before ; but towards the evening I found Christ precious to me, though Satan tempted me to think that it was not the presence of God I enjoyed : but God was stronger than he, and I was not overcome. In the evening, I went to brother Bishop's six o'clock prayer-meeting, and there the Lord poured out his Spirit upon me, and gave me to feel His presence. There were three brethren who prayed exceeding earnestly for sanctification, and gave out suitable hymns, which afforded me great encouragement. When I came home to my closet, upon my bended knees I prayed God to show me His mercies that had been over me all that day; and this he did in a wonderful manner. I thirsted after sanctification, and it was brought to my mind as I was at prayer, ' Blessed are they that hunger and thirst after

righteousness, for they shall be filled;' by which my drooping
soul was greatly cheered."

One of his constitutional infirmities appears to have
been impetuosity of temper; but how much he struggled
against it, and was, by Divine grace, enabled to overcome
it, will appear from the following extracts from his
journal:

"12th September, 1791.—I enjoyed all this day continual
peace with God. In the morning, before I arose, my mind was
composed, and before I went to prayer the second time I found
Christ to be very precious to me. After I came down, the
enemy of my soul strove to overcome me by temptation to
anger, but I could rejoice that I was not overcome. This day
I determined to set out afresh to take the kingdom by force
and violence. In the afternoon, I felt that I did not enjoy so
much of the presence of God as I might do, nor behave myself
with becoming solemnity. In the evening, I was at prayer in
a by-place, where there was some silver-plate, and the enemy
suggested to me how well I might take some of it. Several
times throughout the day he had been busy with me; but God,
who has promised never to leave me nor forsake me, was with
me, and glory be to Him, I enjoyed much of His presence,
could see much of his mercy towards me, and feel inbred sin
to be a burden.

"24th September.—All day I enjoyed continual peace with
God. Before I got out of my bed the Lord broke in upon me,
and I found Christ to be very precious to me, but in the morning it was a miracle of mercy that I was not overcome in
anger, for brother Carey" (his pious fellow-apprentice) "and I
were like to have been stumbling-blocks in each other's way
about a trifling thing, but through mercy (mercy it was) it was
not so. In the afternoon a Jew came into the shop, and a
Baptist professor, and they got into talk with brother Carey
for an hour and a half; but I think he gained nothing by
talking to them. I was almost certain, had I talked to them,
I should have been overtaken in unwatchfulness, and become
angry. At night it was great consolation to me to think that I
was not overtaken in anger all the day, though I was convinced

that there were many things in me that required to be subdued, such as trifling talk, lightness of spirit, and laughter ; but, through mercy, I was not overcome with these this day.

" Sunday, 25th September.—This was a day of mixture. In the morning when I awoke, I found my mind very composed, and I went to our six o'clock prayer-meeting ; but I was tempted greatly against many people who were there, and troubled with wandering thoughts. After that I met my class. After I came out of class-meeting, I tied on a handkerchief round my neck, and I could not arrange it to please me— and how the devil did strive to make me angry in an unwatchful moment ! I could not help weeping. If any carnally-minded persons should read, or hear read this circumstance, they will think it is a mere fable ; but the carnal mind cannot discern the things of the Spirit. They are foolishness to them. In the afternoon I was condemned for being at the house of one of my brothers when I might have been at home at prayer The enemy of my soul went on little by little, for I was pressed upon in the spirit to go many times, but I did not ; I drove it off, minute after minute, as the enemy of souls puts off conversion from the convinced sinner. Thus I was led to consider how dangerous it is to put off anything. Lord have mercy upon me ! for I don't find in any part of the Bible we must repent to-morrow ; no, for that's the devil's time. *Now* is the accepted time, *now, even now*, is the day of salvation. In the evening I was unwell ; and the enemy tempted me not to go to chapel, but I could see from whence the temptation came. I went and enjoyed the presence of God. I met with brother Elliott when I was going to chapel, and we embraced each other with love, and asked after each other's welfare. I told him how my body was, for I was very ill then, and he informed me that his mind was in a very bad state ; so I comforted him as well as I could, and told him I would sooner feel what I did in my body than a wounded conscience. I found it good to wait upon the Lord ; but I had many wandering thoughts after the minister had ended his evening's discourse. He met the society, and told them in a striking manner the danger of neglecting private prayer. After that, I went to see brother Carter, and he thought that because I sighed I was low in spirit, but I told him, no ; I was mourning because I was not more devoted to God, and more given up to Him, so we had a comfortable discourse together for some time. I found myself very happy, my mind being stayed upon God, and my heart lifted up to Him. The hand of the Lord has been over me for good this day. 'God is love!'

"Monday, 26th.—This morning I arose at five o'clock, and went to the preaching. I found a continual peace all day; but towards the afternoon I mourned very much, because I was not more given up to God, and because I had not more religion, or such an earnest desire for holiness as I had in times past. I found myself very humble, and I told brother Carey I was going to set out afresh for Christ's kingdom. Towards night I had some business to do that I did not like, and I found such a peevishness, arising from my own sinful nature, that had I not been watchful I should have been overtaken in anger; but through mercy I was preserved, and did not receive condemnation for it afterwards. I enjoyed the presence of God in a very wonderful manner, and when I laid my body down upon my bed, my mind was in a very composed and peaceable frame. I took a survey of heaven and hell in my thoughts; the joy of one and the misery of the other, and the length thereof, and it stirred me up afresh. Glory be to God for it!

"Tuesday, 27th.—This morning I arose with a peaceable mind. At prayer, Christ broke in upon me, and I enjoyed much of the presence of God all the morning. After dinner, when I was at prayer, the Lord showed me what mercies I enjoyed beyond many others. In the afternoon, I was overtaken with a lightness of spirit, and laughter, though it was not in the sight of man altogether; but yet I knew that God beheld it. I neglected to reprove a greyheaded man for swearing, for which I greatly condemned myself. In the afternoon, I enjoyed so much of the presence of God, that I cried out, Unworthy!—Glory be to God for it! My prayer was, that the Lord would make me even as he would have me to be, and such as he delights to bless.

"Friday, 30th.—Before I got out of my bed this morning, I was convinced that I had been too much like the door upon its hinges, sometimes I was going forward a little, and at another time a little backward. I set out afresh, and indeed it was not in vain, for I enjoyed a continual peace with God all the day long, and received no condemnation, except for not reproving a young woman for taking the Lord's name in vain. I was tempted to anger in the morning, but, through mercy, I was not overcome with it. I enjoyed a great deal more of the presence of God than I had for many days past : my cup ran over with many blessings. I grieved, however, that I had not that earnest desire after sanctification which I had in times past. The enemy of my soul told me it was useless to pray for it, but I did not hearken unto him."

These and many other entries in his diary show how diligently at this early period of his Christian course he searched out his besetting sins, and laboured to bring every thought and purpose of his renewed heart into captivity to the obedience of Christ. And all this was accompanied by earnest and continual prayer, which ascended on the wings of desire ; and whilst his watchful soul waited at heaven's gate for the blessing, the hand of his faith was stretched out until he received it.

It would seem, however, that he often struggled against corruptions in his own strength, instead of looking wholly to Jesus for power to overcome them, and sought for comfort from what was accomplished within him rather than from the finished work of Christ. But these were some of the peculiarities of the school of Divinity to which he belonged, in which the electing love of God, the immutability of His purpose, and the eternal safety of his chosen were lost sight of, or rejected ; and we cannot therefore be surprised that he enjoyed so little of the glorious liberty of the sons of God, and was in perpetual fear of finally falling, and being numbered with the lost.

The following extracts from his diary exhibit the growing spirituality of his mind, and the earnest endeavours he was continually making to adorn the doctrine he professed.

"3rd October, 1791.—Glory be to God for this day's peace, comfort, and consolation! In the morning, at five o'clock, I went to chapel, and as soon as I entered within the door I felt 'this is no other than the house of the Lord,' and I enjoyed much of His presence before the service. During service and afterwards I was mourning after a state of holiness. Satan told me that it was not the will of God, and wanted me to doubt of my justified state; but the Lord showed me by His Spirit what I might have been at that time had it not been for His grace. He showed me likewise my need of humility; but the enemy tried to get an advantage over me. I was tried a great deal with pride and an exalted mind; but I think upon the whole I was kept pretty humble. Through mercy, I enjoyed a great deal of the presence of God and a continual peace all the day except that I was condemned for not living up to my privileges. I think this day I have had more power to reprove sin; I reproved twice and missed once reproving, for which I was condemned. In the afternoon there was an old man, a shoemaker, came to our shop and began swearing, and I reproved him for it; but he made light of it, and began to curse and swear, and abused the poor despised Methodists, one minute profanely calling for the Lord to have mercy upon him, and the next minute calling for damnation. It was a mercy that I was not overcome with anger; but how I was blessed this day! In the evening, about nine o'clock, I was going out on an errand, and hearing a man swearing most bitterly on the other side of the way, I stept across and asked him if he knew he had an immortal soul, and told him he must give an account of those oaths, at which he began swearing and was going to beat me and throw me into the river; but I was not so bold as I ought to have been, being a little afraid. I could see that the devil stirred him up against me, so that I might not reprove sin any more; but I was determined, by the grace of God, not to fear the face of man. Such was my experience this day. Glory be to God.

"7th.—This day I had many struggles with the enemy, who strove to overthrow me with pride, tempting me to an exalted mind, and to say in my heart to my brethren, "Stand thou by for I am more righteous than thou art;" but indeed this had been the case for a long time. I had many trials this day, and was very much tempted to anger many times; but through mercy I was not led captive by him At another time I was tempted to show a spirit of revenge. The enemy was very busy this day; but God's grace was sufficient for me. I was very much afraid that I should fall back again into my former course, but I knew that whilst I had that fear it would go well with me, for if a man were afraid of losing his property, and knew that by watching he should keep it, he would watch: and should not I, whose soul is of so much more consequence, watch?

"15th October, 1791.—I had this day a great trial to weigh my soul down. In the afternoon brother Carey was like to have been a stumbling-block in my way, because he called me names, and when I asked him a question, he answered me so unkindly that it grieved my poor tender heart, for God knew that I desired to be nothing but love. I had talked to him many times, but all to no purpose; I could only pray for him, and this I did, and towards the evening he was more loving, and I was full of love with him, so that we were as happy and as comfortable as ever, and I could rejoice greatly in the God of my salvation. I was sensibly convinced that did we go on so we should lose the power of religion; besides the men made all manner of sport of our religion, so that it was bringing a scandal upon the gospel of Christ, and I was certain we should never bring a soul to God the way we went on.

"21st October, 1791.—This was a blessed day to my soul— a day of comfort. In the morning when I arose my mind was staid on the Lord. In the former part of the afternoon I was very solemn The world seemed quite dead to me, and my mind was engaged in praising God and drinking deeper into the spirit of Christ. Towards the evening I talked more, but not more than I was obliged to do I enjoyed that sweet presence of God which passeth all understanding My trials and temptations have, however, been many, but I found a sweet patience during the former part of the day under my trials. I was tempted to a lightness of spirit in the evening, but through mercy I was not overcome with it. I strove to such a degree to overcome it by the help of God in holding my breath, that my inside was painful to me. The backslider who worked in the shop with me waxed worse and worse ; but the other men thought that the devil was in him. He did not think so once, and I could plainly see that he laboured under convictions, and that his eyes were more opened than they had been. I found Christ very precious to me when I came to spend a little time by myself at night.

"Sunday, 23rd October.—In the morning when I awoke I found my mind in a sweet composed frame, and when I went to prayers I had such a spirit of prayer breathed into my soul that I could pray for everybody, and love even my worst enemies. At the usual time I went to my class-meeting ; and before I went thought I should have a precious time there, but there was something wrong that hindered it, and I seemed quite dead and barren there, though I found no condemnation. Christ broke in upon me once whilst there ; but what was that ? I wanted to receive all He was willing to give me. After it was over I did not seem more alive to God than at first, which caused me to shed tears, I was ashamed to shake hands with ————— that morning, before the worldly people ; but in going to chapel to hear the morning service I met with sister Elliott, and I shook hands with her before them, and the Lord broke in upon my soul in a wonderful manner. If any one should ever read this, I would have them take this for a warning, never to be ashamed of Christ nor yet of His disciples before men, lest Christ should be ashamed of them before His Father and His holy angels. I found Christ precious to my soul in the chapel, and I was humbled under the mighty hand of God. I shed many tears there, upon considering how brother Carey and I lived together, not as Christians nor yet much like worldly people ;—more like beasts ; for there was scarce a day but there was some contrary answer or other passed between us, so that it caused me much sorrow and pain of mind. In the afternoon I went to chapel, and as soon as I fell down upon my knees to ask a blessing upon the word which I was about to hear, Christ broke in upon me in a wonderful manner. I was troubled much with wandering thoughts the former part of the time ; but I cried unto the Lord and he helped me, and afterwards I enjoyed much of the Divine presence. After I came out of the chapel I went with an old warrior, one who had fought many years under the banner of Christ. He told me he dwelt upon the rock, and these words were a blessing to my soul and filled me with joy. After, I talked with more of my brethren, and my soul was enlarged with love. I was not ashamed of my brethren, nor yet of Christ, before men ; and after I parted with them, and got home to my closet, God's love was so poured out upon me that my poor, dull, sinful flesh could scarce contain my soul, nor would it have contained it had there been any means of escape. The Lord still continued to pour out His Spirit upon me all the evening; and after the evening-service I went up to brother Carter, where I enjoyed a few precious moments. We sang part of two hymns, and they were as a fresh meal to my soul. When I was coming away, I desired brother Carter to pray for me, and not to forget me. 'Yea,' said he, 'let my right hand forget her cunning if I forget thee.' So I could bless God at night for that day's experience, and for the love he had bestowed upon me. I could see at night that it was my privilege to enjoy such an experience always as I did that day, so that I set out afresh to take the kingdom of God by more and more violence and watchfulness unto prayer than I ever had done."

In reading what has been just quoted, one is led to say with one of our old divines,—"How true is it that he who has tasted but a little of God's goodness thinks he never has enough of it ; to be sure he can never have too much : there is no fear of surfeiting upon happiness. The least glimpse of God's favourable presence is enough to support and cherish the soul, but it is not enough to satisfy the soul. O how pleasant it is to see Christ flourishing through the lattices ! and yet the spouse will never leave longing till she see Him face to face. There's sweetness indeed in a cluster of Canaan, yet such as set the teeth on edge for more." And such was the state of young Crabb's soul, which daily panted for more of the Divine fulness, as will be seen in the extracts which follow :

"Tuesday, 25th October.—In the morning when I got up, I

found Christ precious to my soul. I was persecuted much throughout the day, but took it with patience. Glory be to God! I was very much troubled with a lightness of spirit; but I was not overcome with it. I was condemned in the morning, for a certain act I committed. Brother Elliott passed by the window, and I told the backslider that Elliott was not liked by many in the society; for which I was condemned, for I had no reason to tell him anything relating to our society. My condemnation would have been greater had I spoken in the presence of the other men, for I had no occasion to tell the faults of the poor Methodists, for the world would find them out fast enough. Brother Carey had lived quite lovingly for two days past, which added to my happiness. In the evening there was a feast kept at my master's house, for the journey-men, and I was considering whether I should go or no; but I thought that I was his servant and that I must obey him, so I went; but before I went in, I prayed God to keep me whilst I was there. It was not much worse to be there than in the shop all the day; so God gave me two promises, many times over, and, glory be to Him, I laid hold of them. The promises were, ' I will never leave thee nor forsake thee,' and ' My grace shall be sufficient for thee ;' and they were a great blessing to my soul; I was wonderfully kept all the time I was there. My mind was in a solemn frame, and Christ was precious to my soul. They wondered why brother Carey and I were so solemn, and as the apostle Paul says, 'thought it strange that we did not run with them to the same excess of riot,' for which we were laughed at and ridiculed; but that availed nothing to hurt our precious souls. Brother Carey and I came away before the rest of the men, and made a solemn determination, by the grace of God, to be more and more in earnest to love each other, and to let our light shine before men. So we parted very lovingly; and for my part, I don't know when I found Christ so precious to my soul. There was one thing that happened that evening which I felt very much ; it was the backslider's singing songs. He had a fine voice and could sing very well. I thought upon old times, when he used to be praising God with that voice; but now it was employed in the devil's service, so that it went to my heart.

"Wednesday, 26th October.—In the morning when I arose I found my mind stayed on the Lord, and enjoyed much of His presence all the day; I was, however, troubled much with a lightness of spirit, but was not, through mercy, overcome by it. Brother Carey and I lived very lovingly together all the day, which was a great happiness and comfort to my soul, and I was warned of God that day, whilst watching my outward actions, to beware of my foes within—pride, anger, and malice—and, glory be to God, it stirred me up in some measure. We were much persecuted by the backslider, and heard all manner of sinful language proceed from his mouth all day long; but towards the evening brother Carey got talking of very solemn things, which touched the backslider's conscience; but Collins was worse and worse.

"Friday, 4th November.—In the morning, I found Christ precious to my soul, though before breakfast a few words slipped out of my mouth, for which I was condemned, though it was some time before I could acknowledge it to be a sin. However, I repented of it and found pardon. Brother Carey told me he feared that the enemy of my soul was getting advantage over me, little by little; and the worst of it was, that the worldly people in the shop spoke well of me, and it was like a dagger to my heart. How I wept all the remainder of the evening, for fear I should leave my God and He should then forsake me! No pen or tongue can express what agony of soul I found, lest I should get cold in the ways of God. I cried out within myself, 'What! can I leave my Jesus?' Then a fresh flood of tears flowed from my eyes. Collins made fun of me afterwards, but I told him that they were tears that never would be forgotten to all eternity. I prayed much in the morning, and looked back upon that part of the week that had been spent, and I could give but little account of my enjoyment of God, though it was much greater than I deserved, but little to what I might have enjoyed; all which tended to stir me up, and when I came to cry to God for mercy, on account of my offences, he granted it, and gave me so much love that I could not help weeping for joy. I was tempted twice not to meet in class any more, that I might not be obliged to confess my faults. I bore a particular love towards brother Carey afterwards, and he to me, and I very affectionately desired him to pray for me at night, when we parted from our daily labour. I could see it a great mercy, all the afternoon, that I was out of hell; indeed, no pen or tongue can express what I went through this day.

"Sunday, 20th November.—I awoke about five o'clock this morning, to the joy of my soul, and having struck a light, went to prayer. Christ cheered my drooping spirit, and quickened and kindled in me a zeal for true religion. After this I went to a public prayer meeting, where the Lord was with me; afterwards I had a walk with brother Smith. Our talk was not earthly, but heavenly—our conversation was in some measure as becometh the gospel of Christ. I left him and went to sister Hayter's house; we went to meet in class together. I found my mind stayed on God whilst I was there, though I was condemned by my own heart for not telling brother Higton, the class-leader, the whole of my experience of my unworthiness and sinfulness; for whilst I was in the class I could see many sins I had committed during the past week which I did not see before. The Apostle James tells us in the fifth chapter of his epistle, and at the sixteenth verse, that we should confess our faults one to another, and pray for one another, that we may be healed. The effectual fervent prayer of a righteous man availeth much; and through not so doing I brought much darkness over my soul for a few moments. I asked forgiveness of the Lord, and he granted it; afterwards I found my soul very much drawn out after God, and was humbled. In the morning sermon, preached by brother Alger, I was greatly stirred up; I saw myself wanting in many things, and that there was much in me that was displeasing in God's sight. In the afternoon I felt more of my sinfulness than ever; but I set out twice that day with a determination to know more of the things that appertained to my soul's interest— to be watchful over my deceitful heart, the allurements of the world, the temptations of the devil—to know more of Christ Jesus—to have His image stamped more and more on my soul, and to grow up into Him; and I did not doubt but that, by the grace of God, I should be more watchful. It is good to set out in the strength of the Lord. In the evening I went to see the corpse of the young man (whom I went to see the Sunday before) put into the earth, and under the funeral ceremonies I found a very solemn sense of the presence of God. It was good to be there. Afterwards I went to chapel, where my soul was humbled and much drawn out after God, and I enjoyed much of His love in the evening. I saw Collins there in the morning, and he was there, too, in the afternoon. It did my soul good to see him, and I almost burst out in praising God aloud in the chapel for His goodness in bringing him there. There were many people there that evening who I knew were in some measure awakened, which did me good. I was full of love in the evening, and begged the Lord to awake me early in the morning, that I might rise to praise him. After I got into bed I said, ' O God, into thy hand I commit myself, body, soul, and spirit, and do thou awake me early in the morning, for I cannot awake myself.' His answer was, ' I will grant thee the desire of thy heart ;' and with this answer I fell asleep in the arms of my Jesus.

" Friday, 30th December, 1791.—In the morning oblation I found Christ very precious to my soul, and I enjoyed much of His love. In the fore part of the day Satan tempted me very much to pride of a spiritual nature. In the evening I was observing to brother Carey what happiness it was to me that we had lived together in love, as we had during the last six weeks. We bear with each other's infirmities, and strive to bear each others burdens in all things, so that the men in the shop could not find fault with us as they used to do. Brother Carey was convinced he used to give way to his ill tempers too much, so that we each strive, with a determination, by the grace of God, to live more and more lovingly than ever. In the evening I was more happy than I had been for some time ; yea, I almost seemed to double in happiness day by day, and I found great life and liberty in prayer, and very great promises, upon which I seemed to lay hold, by the help of God. I could see the mercy of God that night in giving me His love, as he did, so that my days seemed to be full of peace and joy in the Holy Ghost. I had a glorious thirsting that evening after holiness, to the glory of God and to the joy of my soul."

CHAPTER III.

Grace in the heart.—Decision for God.—Diary.—Extracts from it.
—Review of his past career.—His progress in the divine life.

FROM the preceding extracts we see something of those
developments of grace in the heart which cannot be mistaken. " Grace," says holy Robert Bolton, " is like leaven
(for so the power of God's word is compared in the
Gospel) ; it is of a spreading nature. First, it seats itself
in the heart ; after, it is dispersed over all the powers and
parts, both of soul and body—over all the actions and
duties of a man whatsoever. It softeneth and changeth
the heart ; it purgeth the inmost thoughts ; it awakens
the conscience, and makes it tender and sensible of the
least sin ; it sanctifies the affections ; it conforms the will
unto the will of God ; it enlightens the understanding
with saving knowledge ; it stores the memory with many
good lessons, for comforts, instructions, and directions in
a godly life ; it seasons the speech with grace ; it so
rectifies and guides all a man's actions, that they proceed
from faith ; they are warrantable out of God's word ; they
are accomplished by good means, and wholly directed to
the glory of God. Nay, yet it spreads further, and kindles
a desire of zeal for the salvation of the souls of others,
especially of all those that any way depend upon us ; so
that the child of God doth ever embrace all means and

opportunities for the communicating of his graces and comforts, and the bringing of others to the same state of happiness with himself."—*Bolton's Discourse on True Happiness, p.* 84. And all this had begun to manifest itself in the daily walk and experience of our young neophyte, who had now discovered, that there is in the Christian's life, however many his trials, and however great his conflicts, a blessedness which is full of glory, and a joy with which a stranger does not intermeddle, and which can no more be described than the sweetness of the honey-comb can be painted.

In entering upon the year 1792, he appears to have set out with full purpose of heart to reach forth unto those things which were before him, and how zealously he did so is apparent from the daily entries which he made in his diary.

On the first day of that year he writes :

" As soon as I awoke, I felt the mercy of God in sparing me to another year, and I determined, by the grace of God, to live more in union with Christ, and to do more of His will. In the morning I joined with my class, and found it good to wait upon the Lord. After that I went to church and received the sacra-ment, at which I had a solemn sense of the goodness of the Lord towards me. In the afternoon I went to chapel, and then the enemy tempted me very much, and my own heart tried to deceive me, too, by looking for the praise of men ; but my soul hated it, and I tried to mortify it as much as I could. In the evening I felt the preciousness of Christ, and wanted to fly away and be at rest. I had a very comfortable conversation after preaching, with one of my sisters ; my way seemed easy that night ; but I did not expect that it would be always so, for I was convinced that if I was no cross-bearer I should be no crown-wearer, and I was certain that it would be through much tribulation that I should enter the kingdom of heaven.

" 28th January.—When I arose I found Christ precious to

my soul, and, to the glory of God's grace, I enjoyed much of His love all the day, more especially in the evening. God was drawing my affections from this present world to things above. I could truly say, by His assistance, that the world and all things therein seemed entirely under my feet, and I saw such an ocean of love open before me, that it filled my raptured soul with intense love to all my brethren. I saw a poor traveller in the evening, who inquired of me for lodgings, and I could not help praying for him when I went before the Lord. I had not so many temptations this day as I had the day before; but I found that the devil was not dead. I think I felt my own unworthiness this day in a great measure. I was taking notice likewise what great things the Lord had done for my soul, though I had been in the ways of God a twelvemonth only this very day. That pious man, Joseph Alger, admitted me into the Methodist Society, which was a few days after I set out to fear God.

"Tuesday, 31st January.—I arose this morning before five o'clock, and I found it a profitable time to my precious soul. I determined to press on towards the kingdom, and to redouble my diligence; and by the grace and assistance of God, I was enabled to put it in practice this day by living much more solemnly. I found my mind in a solid steady frame all the day, having a constant reliance upon God; but the devil told me I was deceiving myself. I was certain, however, that he was a liar, and the father of lies, so he did not disturb my peace. I had not so many temptations this day as I have had before. In the evening I went up to brother Bishop's, and there, in a particular manner, I found myself the unworthiest of the unworthy, so that I could not help shedding tears. I found a very humbling, solemn sense of the Lord's presence all the time, and was greatly stirred up to redouble my diligence, and to live closer to the fountain that never did or will dry up. I thirsted for a greater work to be completed in my soul, which I have no doubt the Lord will accomplish.

"February, 1792.—I rose this morning before five o'clock, my desires increased, and after I had done writing, the devil tempted me to go to bed again, but I did not hearken unto him, and continued reading. I was glad I did not go to bed, for my whole soul was filled with love. I don't know that I ever enjoyed so blessed a morning before. It is impossible to express the desires and thirstings I had. I was never so drawn out after God. I wanted to be swallowed up in Him, and to know nothing but Christ. The devil found it was not of much use to preach unbelief to me, and therefore he strove to prop me up with pride; but through mercy, I was enabled to withstand him, and to look to Jesus. After I went down stairs I found my mind stayed on God, and I could truly say that I could be content with nothing but Jesus, who was all that I had, and all that I wanted. I knew that I could derive no comfort from any other spring than from God through Christ Jesus.

"Thursday.—Rose at my usual hour, between four and five, and I found it good to wait upon the Lord. What blessings and privileges I enjoy! I have no one to disturb me. What comfort I find in reading and prayer every morning! I first return God thanks for the preservation of the night past, then I read a chapter or two, and then a hymn or two, and then commit myself into the hands of God by prayer for the day. I find my room a little heaven below. By this I am strengthened for the day before me, and prepared for many temptations; and this is what I get by rising before light. I was very much drawn out after God all this day, and through mercy I was enabled to go on with joy and rejoicing.

"3rd March, 1792.—In prayer my soul was drawn out after God, and I found his presence in a blessed manner. I had many trials this day, but I had much of God's love all the day long. I was tempted very much to do things contrary to the will of God, and Satan had many hard struggles at my soul to make me give way to him; but God was my helper and my deliverer.

"Wednesday, 11th March.—This was such a day as I never knew before. It was nothing but happiness and ravishing joys, I rose before it was light to wait upon the Lord; but the devil wanted to cheat me by persuading me not to get up so soon, for he does not like the saints of the Most High to rise early; but the Lord hath said, 'them that seek me early shall find me.' I found Christ to be the joy of, and very precious, to my soul. I had a fervent desire to get a cleansed heart. About

nine o'clock in the morning I believed, and entered into rest
for these words came to my mind very powerfully, as an arrow
from a bow : ' If thou canst believe, all things are possible unto
thee ;' and from that moment I laid hold on the promise, to the
glory of God and to the joy of my soul. No tongue or pen can
express what a day I passed. There was not, to my knowledge,
any unbelief remaining ; but Satan tempted me to think, that
there was no occasion to get so much grace, or to attain to so
high a degree ; but I did not mind him. I could say with David
of old, 'Come, all ye that fear the Lord, and I will tell you
what he hath done for my soul. I was however tempted to
spiritual pride ; but I firmly believed that the Lord had spread
abroad his sanctifying influences in my soul, and that he would
carry on the work to the end, did I but hold fast. Glory be
to God, the temptations of Satan seemed nothing, though they
were very strong. This I have written to the glory of God,
not taking it to myself. This was my cry all the day,

> ' The promised land, from Pisgah's top,
>   I now exult to see.
> My hope is full ; oh, glorious hope
>   Of immortality !'

" 13th March.—This was a refreshing day to my soul, but it
was a trying day. I rose before it was light, and had a refreshing time from heaven to my precious soul, and, glory be to
God, I found great desires and determinations to go forward ;
but the devil tried to distress my soul most heavily all the
day in various ways. He tempted me to unbelief, and used
every artifice imaginable to destroy my liberty. Sometimes
he made me uneasy, but I went to the Lord, and poured out
my complaint to Him, and found Him a God hearing and a
God answering prayer. Glory be to his name ! I did not bow
before him once this day without finding, through mercy,
Christ very precious to my soul. In the evening, I had an
extraordinary thirsting after all the mind that was in Christ ;
but it was impossible for me to express the love that was
showered down upon me this night. My faith was strengthened. I did not seem to have a doubt but that God would do
that great work of holiness in a sure manner, and in a short

time, were I but faithful. Through mercy, God was my support all the day, so that I could truly say,

> ' A vile backslider, I,
> Ten thousand deaths deserve to die ;
>   Yet still by sovereign grace I live ;
> Saviour, to thee, I still look up,
> I see an open door of hope,
>   And wait thy fulness to receive.' "

On the 10th December, 1792, upon reviewing the state of his heart, he writes :

" I found the Lord deepening his work in my soul, and that I had more of the mind of Christ ; though, alas ! I found little of what I ought to have found. I was ashamed before God that I had made no greater progress in the Divine life. I felt that every one was advancing but me, and determined to seek to have the kingdom of God more displayed in my soul.

" I felt that if I had nothing but my own wisdom, I was certainly a fool; but, blessed be God! I find that he is teaching me wisdom day by day. As clay lies in the hands of the potter, so do I desire to lie in the hands of my God.

" I found the Lord's promise fulfilled this day, that those who wait upon Him shall renew their strength. I was all the day filled with desires ; I wanted to be swallowed up in Christ, and to be entirely moulded into God's image."

On the 28th January, 1793, being the day on which the second year of his connection with the Methodists terminated, he thus speaks of himself and the progress he had made in his Christian course :

" I find that the Lord has, in a peculiar manner, deepened his work in my soul. I can truly say, by the grace of God, through Jesus Christ, that I can rejoice with that joy which is unspeakable, and full of glory. But what a poor, dependent creature I am upon the mercy and grace of God. May my whole delight be, to serve the Lord with all my heart."

Whilst these extracts present a striking example of youthful piety and self-consecration to God, they contain much that is valuable in reference to Christian life and practice, which may not be altogether unprofitable to the reader. That the views young Crabb had formed of the covenant of grace were in some respects erroneous, and consequently that he was often under the spirit of bondage, is manifest; but his heart was right with God. There was the honest aim, the single eye; his face was Zionward, and Christ was precious to him; and where all this is found, mistakes will in due time be rectified. Whatever his defects may have been, his Diary manifestly shows that he knew the difference between the religion of water-baptism and the religion which springs from regeneration by the Spirit; in other words, the religion of profession and the religion of the heart, and exhibits the great truth that "the grace of God teaches its recipients to deny ungodliness and worldly lusts, and to live soberly, righteously, and godly in this present world." To one brought into this happy condition, "we need not," says Culverwell, "use many persuasions. It has a fountain of rhetoric within. There is a present expansion and amplification of spirit for the welcoming of so happy an object. O! how will such a soul twine about a precept—suck sweetness out of a command—catch at an opportunity—long for a duty,—how does it go, like a bee, from flower to flower, from duty to duty, from ordinance to ordinance, and exhaust the very spirit and quintessence of all—crop the very tops of all. There will be in such a soul the constant returnings and reboundings of love; it will retort the beams of heaven; it will send back the stream of its affection into the ocean, so that now, as the soul is assured of the love of God, so God also has a most absolute certainty that the soul will Αντιφιλειν ; and thus is completed the sweet and perfect circle of love."

Dear reader, he who is continually thinking of her whom he loves, who talks of her, and would not allow her perfections, real or imaginary, to be disparaged, will not be blamed, but rather admired; but he who loves God, thinks of Him, talks of Him, sighs for Him, pants after Him, and would see Him honoured by all men, is accounted a fool, or an enthusiast.   Oh, when shall this world be wholly peopled by such fools and enthusiasts !

CHAPTER IV.

At the time when young Crabb connected himself with the Wesleyans, there was little vital religion to be found in any class of society. The Church of England had fallen into a deep slumber. The unhallowed influence of the State had corrupted her manners, sullied her purity, and paralyzed her energies. Her beautiful garments had become polluted with the filth of this world; she reflected little of the image of Christ; and a lifeless morality had been substituted for the soul-quickening and life-giving truths of the Gospel. Those amongst her clergy who professed and preached evangelical truth, and they were few in number, were branded as enthusiasts, or Methodists, and became the subjects of reproach and persecution. So early as the year 1757, when blessed Romaine preached two sermons before the University of Oxford, at St. Mary's and St. Peter's, on the " Righteousness of the Believer, as derived from Christ," they were so offensive to the "divines" of that seat of learning, that he was thenceforth excluded from the University pulpit, and the same antipathy to evangelical religion still prevailed.

But whilst there was little or no religion in any class of society, the moral state of the lower classes was little better than that of heathen lands. There was little or no education among them. There were at that time no Sabbath-schools, no visiting, no tract, no Bible societies, city or town missionaries or Scripture-readers, nor much, if any, domiciliary visitation amongst the poor; and none of the religious societies, which during the last fifty years have done so much for the population of London and the provinces, had any existence. By far the greater proportion of the religion of the country was to be found amongst the despised and persecuted followers of Wesley and Whitefield; and we have a sample of what was and could be accomplished by individual effort, in the Diary from which the preceding extracts have been made.

Young Crabb had not been associated much more than two years with the followers of Wesley before he began to feel a deep concern for the many, whose souls no man seemed to regard. Being easily led away by his feelings, he often acted without judgment and fell into great indiscretions; and one of his greatest mistakes was that of becoming, at this period of his life, a preacher. That his heart was right with God, and that he felt a deep concern for souls, cannot be doubted; but he had little of the experience and knowledge required for so solemn and momentous an employment. Being yet in his apprenticeship, the only opportunities he had of preaching were on the Sabbath days on which he was free. His first attempt as a preacher was made when he was between eighteen and nineteen years of age, in a chalk-pit, at Coombe, in the Blandford-road, when he spoke from Rom. v. 19. He has left a record of the event, in which he says : " I was not ashamed of the face of any man, and I stood up before many, some of whom had been my school-fellows, and proclaimed to them the way of salvation." This he continued to do for several Sabbaths, notwithstanding many hindrances and much opposition. His master having become acquainted with his Sabbath exercises, persecuted him with great rigour, and his father was so incensed that he ceased all intercourse with him, withdrew his allowance of pocket-money, and threatened, unless he desisted, to discard him altogether. None of these things, however, moved him, for believing that he was in the path of duty, he continued to preach. In this matter, however, he greatly erred; for, being under parental authority, it was his duty to submit to the will of his father.

Having preached for some Sabbaths at Coombe, he went to the adjoining parish of Hamnington, where the common people flocked to hear him. On one occasion, however, the minister of the parish and one of the farmers threatened, upon his coming there again, to place him in the stocks. Nothing daunted, he proceeded on the next Sabbeth to Hamnington, with two or three pious companions; and upon his arrival at the place where he was to preach, found a constable, who, being instructed not to interfere unless there was a disturbance, did not molest him. He preached from, " Fear God. Honour the King," 1 Pet. ii. 17 ; and called upon his hearers to testify whether he said anything calculated to lead to a breach of the peace or a violation of the law. The people listened with silence ; and instead of spending the evening in the stocks (for which he was fully prepared, and in the expectation of which he had provided extra clothing to keep himself warm), he returned home in peace. These Sabbath services were soon noised abroad; and as his natural talents, Scripture knowledge, and fluency of utterance were not contemptible, he began to acquire considerable fame; and his father, seeing that it was in vain to oppose the settled purpose of his mind, and being softened by the dutiful letters he received from him, withdrew his opposition; a circumstance which gave a new impetus to his efforts. His success at this period will be best told in his own words:

"My preaching, as it was called, was soon noised abroad, and having been invited to Ford, I accordingly went, and the presence of God went with me. I took for my text, 'My people are destroyed for lack of knowledge,' and the Lord was pleased, by His Spirit, to shine not only in my heart, but on the word; and from that time I never wanted understanding in the word, or language in speaking. My calls to preach were now universal, as far as the influence of Methodism prevailed, and being without experience, my first plans were adopted under the advice of Mr. Catman, by whom I was brought under control. Seeing now my way clear, and believing I was called of God to preach the Gospel, I did so with all my heart. I bought myself an oil-lawn umbrella, which cost me in those days twenty shillings, by which I was enabled to brave all weathers, and to be ready for duty on all occasions. Never did I miss a duty which my poorer brethren could not perform. My walks were generally from ten to thirty miles on the Sunday. I used to start before breakfast, and take my bread and cheese in my pocket. Oh, the happy hours I have enjoyed with my God in these duties! In my long journeys, I used to finish my Sabbath duties in my native town, Wilton, three miles from my master's house at Salisbury, and on these occasions I always had my dear mother as one of my congregation, and, dear soul, she soon was enlightened by the word of God. In

c 3

this long circuit, I came across the Downs from Chalk to Barford, where I met a good congregation. One Sabbath day, after preaching, the good minister of the parish came out to meet me, and asked what I had been about ? when I told him I had been preaching the Gospel. Having asked me for my authority, I replied, that my authority was from God. He then asked me where I was educated, and I told him, in *Christ's college*. Whether he understood my meaning, I know not, but being a simple-hearted man, he did not try me with more questions.

"The next important place I went to was Whitefarish, seven miles from Salisbury. Here lived some very judicious hearers, amongst whom was the school-master of the parish, a sensible man, who was of great service to me : but here my pride was much fed, for the people, thinking I was a very clever youth, praised me to my face, and I received and believed every word they spoke. One circumstance greatly helped to increase my vanity. A young man accompanied me to this place, and on our return home, he was in great distress of mind on account of his sins, and we turned out of the road on the hill and offered prayer to God, who, whilst we were thus engaged, gave him the assurance that his sins were pardoned. How did I bound my way home ! not humbled under the mighty hand of God, as I ought to have been, but lifted up with the thought that it was by my prayer he was restored ; nor were the silly people less in their praises when the circumstance was known."

Having continued these Sabbath-services for about two years, our young preacher began to entertain the idea, that he was called to devote himself wholly to the work of the ministry. Although a follower of Wesley, he was attached to the Church of England, and highly esteemed its liturgy and articles ; but, however much he might desire to labour within its pale, and however great might be his spiritual gifts, his want of learning excluded him from its precincts. But, happily for many, he was not living under the law which excluded a Bunyan from the pulpit, and although the door of one Church was closed against him, the doors of other churches, which estimated men by their graces and not by their learning—by their spiritual, and not by their human attainments, were open to him.

Having fully determined to give himself up to the work of the Lord, he forthwith set about removing the obstacles which were in his way; the greatest of which was, that there were yet eighteen months of his apprenticeship unexpired, during the continuance of which he could preach on the Sabbath only   This difficulty, however, he soon overcame, for having succeeded in raising twenty pounds, his master, upon receipt of that sum, released him from further service. This took place in the month of April, 1794, and in the month of February, 1795, he offered himself to the Wesleyan Conference, as a preacher; and after passing through the usual ordeal, he was accepted, and shortly after received an appointment as an itinerant supply-preacher for the district of Poole, Swannage, and the Isle of Portland. Taking into consideration his youth—he being yet under the age of twenty-one years—this appointment would seem to reflect little credit on those by whom it was made; but it must be borne in mind, that at that time there was a great work to be done amongst the lower classes of the people; the harvest was great, and the labourers were few; and it was no light matter to reject a lay-preacher because of his youth, when he was qualified for the work he had to do   That he entered upon the work with a heart wholly surrendered to God and burning with love to souls, there can be no doubt, and though young and inexperienced, he was in His hands who could overrule all his mistakes for good, reprove him by his follies, and make "all grace abound towards him."

It was on the 6th March, 1795, that he began his

course on the circuit to which he had been appointed, and in the Diary which he then commenced he thus speaks of himself and the labours upon which he had now entered:

"I had one competent qualification for a minister, and that was the love of souls. I entered on my work in the name of the Lord, and did not do it by halves. I preached every morning at five o'clock, and every evening in the week, beside five times on the Lord's day when in Portsmouth, exclusive of the seven o'clock prayer meeting, and the meeting of the society for wholesome advice, or a love feast. My times for preaching were three times in the two chapels, and twice out of doors, one of the latter being to seamen in Bath-square. I used to think on my dear mother's words, which were, 'James, I wonder your tongue does not ache;' and truly after my Sunday work, in the evening, my tongue has literally ached. It was a very extensive circuit; it embraced the whole of the Isle of Wight, extended as far into the Andover Circuit as within nine miles of Newbury, in Berks, namely, at Banghurst, and within fifteen miles of Salisbury to Timsbury. Then in the east of Portsmouth we had what was called a mission, which ran up within little less than thirty miles of London. On this mission we had some tremendously long walks. We took in Chichester, Arundel, then struck across the Sussex downs to Storrington, where we had a kind of Irish cabin to rest at."

Some idea of his abundant labours may be formed, when it is stated that on traversing the Surrey and Sussex part of his circuit, he had between 3 and 400 miles to walk in six weeks, at a time, too, when he was far from being strong. From entries in his Diary, he appears one day to have walked twenty-seven, another thirty, and another forty miles, in order to reach his place of destination. On Monday, the 13th April, 1795, being the day on which he attained his majority, he thus writes in his Diary:—

"Since the 10th April, 1794 (in which calculation he includes his labours prior to his appointment as a preacher), I have

walked in journeys in the cause of God more than 1,300 miles
ridden above 800, and made voyages of 100 miles. Lord what
am I that thou art mindful of me, or deignest to visit me! I
have now been a servant of God between four and five years,
and a preacher between two and three; but alas! how few of
my days have been really devoted to God."

The character of the labours in which he was now engaged, and the trials he had to encounter, are, together
with the experience he derived from them and the help
they afforded him in the Divine life, fully detailed by him
in his Diary, from which the following extracts have been
made, in the hope that whilst they are not destitute of
interest, they may not be unprofitable to the spiritual
reader :

"Friday, 19th June, 1795.—I arose about four in the morning
(after having had little rest during the night), intending to go
to Godalming, a distance of twenty-nine miles. As it was a
most wet and cold morning, I wanted to go inside the coach;
but there being no room, my friends, as I was very poorly,
would not let me go outside. This was the first time I ever
disappointed a congregation through wet weather, and God
grant it may be the last, for I was not satisfied in my mind all
the day. In the evening I was so very ill that I could scarcely
walk.

"Saturday, 20th June—Notwithstanding the weak state of
my body, I set out between seven and eight in the morning,
intending that day, if possible, to walk near thirty miles. It
was so cold a day (though the 20th of June), that I was obliged
to put my hands into my bosom many times to get heat That
day, owing to the cold, scores of swallows were taken up dead,
and hundreds of sheep that had been shorn, died with the cold
The wind was so strong (though we had two days rain successively), that in about ten hours it caused the dust to fly
The wind being right against me, and I being weak, could at
times hardly creep along; once it was so powerful that it blew
me against some rails, by which I was alone saved from falling
How good is the Lord still unto such a dust as I am, Lord,

help me to love thee more and serve thee better ! The first mile I walked I was very tired ; but I soon got a little strength. When I had walked about twelve miles, I was so tired and faint that I hardly knew how I should get on. I seated myself under a hedge, and having put up my umbrella to keep off the wind, took out my bread and cheese (having bought a penny loaf in Chichester), and prayed God to bless it to the strengthening of my body, and to feed my soul with hidden manna. O! how greatly was my soul blessed ! I was for a season as in heaven, though under a hedge. I could say, Lo ! God is here indeed. O ! my God, give me more gratitude, for how little do I love thee ! My body was also blessed, for I got up as strong as though I had not walked a mile. I went the remainder of my journey rejoicing and praising God. My food this day was angels' food. When I got a little weary, I again sat down a few minutes under a warm hedge, and thereby increased my strength. I had a complete fulfilment of the promise of God, ' As thy day is so shall thy strength be.' I felt very thankful when I arrived at my journey's end, which was about half-past four in the evening. O God, when shall I be more lost in wonder, but, above all, in love and praise !

" Sunday, 21st.—I arose (though very stiff and poorly) early, and preached in the forenoon, my soul being watered from on high. After dinner I rode five miles (for I could not walk, I had so great a pain in my side), where I preached in the afternoon and evening. I felt much for precious souls this day, and found it good to be employed for the Lord, and in his vineyard. O ! that I was more faithful !

" Tuesday, 23rd June.—This day I had to go from Hammer Ponds to Portsmouth, which is thirty-four miles,—twelve I rode and twenty-two I walked. I filled my pockets with two penny loaves and two pennyworth of cheese, and with these I marched on. I can truly say I fed on Jesus all the way. My soul was enlarged with God, and I was enabled to rejoice ; but I want to love the God of my strength more.

" Sunday, 28th.—I arose this morning for the prayer-meeting, and it was a comfortable season to my soul. I felt a gracious time this morning in preaching. In the afternoon I had to ride six miles, through a heavy rain, to preach. I was importuned to stay at home ; *but I remembered the* 19*th of June,* and I ventured forth, and having got wet to my skin, I was obliged to remain until I went to bed, for I had no clothes for a change. I preached and had a good time. I was very poorly and weak in body most of this day. In the morning, when I came from the prayer-meeting, I was obliged to go to bed again, and when I returned from the country I was so overpowered with fatigue (being so weak), that I laid myself down until preaching time in the evening. At six o'clock I preached in Newport chapel, and my soul was watered from on high in a gracious manner. Lord, what am I, or what is my father's house, that thou art thus mindful of me ! When shall I be given up entirely to God ? *Now,* Lord !

"Monday, 29th.—When I arose this morning, I was quite stiff from the fatigue of the preceding day ; but glory be to God, I felt my soul drawn out unto and after Him. Lord, I am sensible that I love thee little ; let this be the time when my whole soul shall be swallowed up in thee. This evening I preached in Newport, and felt a good time. Would to God I preached more by *example !*

"Tuesday, 30th, 1795.—I had many visits from the Lord. O God ! how great is thy love.

> ' Whence to me this waste of love !
>   Ask my Advocate above ;
>   See the cause in Jesus' face,
>   Now before the throne of grace.'

It was extremely wet to-day, and I had four miles to walk. I had many reasonings on my mind about going ; but I was determined, by the help of God, to go, and I did. Through fatigue a fever has come on; but God makes amends for it by giving me a very joyful soul. My health seems now to be low ; I have not only a fever, but little appetite, and get little sleep ; but, blessed be God, when I don't sleep, I lay and praise Him, and for hours think on his Word ; so that I prove in my experience that everything works together for good, and in everything I am enabled to give thanks. Oh, my God, why is not my whole soul swallowed up in thee ! ' As the hart panteth for the water brooks, so panteth my soul after thee, O God.'

"Sunday, July 5th.—I arose early, though I had little sleep; I felt a nearness to God in prayer this morning. At seven o'clock I went to the prayer-meeting, where the Lord was with me, and blessed me. At half-past ten, I preached from 'Ye are dead, and your life is hid with Christ in God.' It was a most glorious time to my soul, and whilst speaking of sanctification and a death unto sin, I could set to my seal unto the truth of it. In the afternoon I preached from Jabez' prayer, 'O! that Thou wouldst bless me, indeed,' &c. I felt liberty of soul, and much zeal for precious souls. After tea, in the afternoon (being fatigued), I laid myself down on the bed for a little rest, and O, my God, how didst thou bless my soul! I was surely within the veil. God was discovered, and felt by me. I was lost in astonishment at his visiting such a worm as I am. Heaven, indeed, came down to my soul. As fast as I prayed God answered; and while I was praising, fresh mercies came down. My whole soul was filled with prayer, and love for precious souls. I was in a wrestling agony for them.

"At six o'clock this evening, I went into the chapel, and in singing and prayer I felt great power. I preached from Naaman the leper, 2 Kings, chap. v., and part of the thirteenth verse, 'My Father,' &c. Surely Christ did preach that night, and God was in our midst. I doubt not there were this night many souls convinced by God under the word. Lord suffer not the devil to take away the seed sown in their hearts. I closed the day with my heart filled with God; and in my bed, until twelve o'clock, I laid and praised Him. Lord, make me more humble and more holy.

"12th July, 1795.—This morning I arose early, and went to the prayer-meeting. I found that the Lord was in our midst. At nine o'clock, I preached out of doors; and at half-past ten, in the chapel, and had a remarkable time. At one o'clock I preached at Portsmouth Point to harlots and sailors. A very large congregation I had; and they were as quiet as though it had been under a roof. I felt that the Lord had the hearts of all men in his hands. At half-past two, I preached in Oyster-street Chapel to a large congregation, from the parable of the sower. At six, I preached in the Bishop-street Chapel from 'Strive to enter in at the strait gate.' Afterwards I met the Society, and was faithful to their souls. I concluded the day with much thanksgiving to God for his mercies. This day my little body went through much labour , I preached five times, read the Church service once, met the Society, and attended the prayer-meeting . and yet I found myself fresh, and almost fit for another day. Oh God, thy mercies will never end ! The following week I preached twice almost every day, at five in the morning and seven in the evening. In preaching the word of eternal truth, the last week, I found my soul much watered from on high, and I have felt my zeal and love enlarged ; but, Lord, when shall I be more zealous ? I have had this past week many close attacks from Satan, which I have keenly felt ; but I know that God is my deliverer. Lord, what a mercy that thou art mindful of me I feel at times great sorrow of soul that I am not found more faithful Sure I am there are none so unfaithful as I am ; but, blessed be God, I do hold fast my shield. I find it is heaven to love and dwell in Jesus ; but, oh ! Lord, when shall I love thee better ? Thou, Lord, knowest my chief desire is to love thee ! where is there, Lord, an object, or a darling, that I cannot give up for thee ? But, oh, Lord, when will my soul be made more alive—when shall I be filled with the whole fulness of God ? Lord, do I not love thee more this moment that ever I did ? Oh, keep me, and never let me go. Fill me, O my Saviour ! with thy love, and make my heart to run over with praise

"Sunday, 25th July.—I arose early and committed myself and made known my wants, unto the Lord. I had a great day's work before me, but God, even my God, was greater than the work. At seven in the morning, I went to the prayer-meeting ; I felt it good to be there. At nine o'clock, I preached out of doors. At half-past ten, I preached in the chapel, and the Lord visited a poor worm still with his mercy. At half-past one, I preached again out of doors on the Portsmouth Point to the woman and sailors. I had as many as I could make hear, and a very peaceable time it was Many wept bitterly, and one woman in particular I had a most glorious time, and felt it very hard to leave them. At half-past two, I preached in the Oyster-street Chapel, and had a

large congregation. At six, I preached again. A most blessed
time I had; the Lord seemed to keep good wine until the last.
At half-past seven, I held a prayer-meeting in a public-house
in Portsmouth, and a good time we had; and thus I concluded
the day, after having seen and felt much of the mercy and
love of God to my soul, and the souls of others. Oh, my God,
when shall I love and serve thee better.

"Sunday, 2nd August.—I again laboured in Portsmouth.
At nine o'clock I preached out of doors. It rained a great
part of the time, but the congregation stood it very well without running away. It was a good time to my soul, and much
good I believe the Lord did there, first and last. Many who
were notorious sinners, and some who were persecutors, were
brought to hear the Word in the chapel. Would to God I
were more diligent in street and field preaching. I see, in one
sense, that the salvation of many souls depends on it. At
half-past ten, I read prayers, and preached in Bishop-street
Chapel. I had a good time to my soul. At half-past one, I
preached down on the Point to the women and sailors. They
were very serious in general. There was one I saw take up a
stone, and run with great haste towards me. I looked at him
very hard, and he soon slank away with the stone in his bosom.
On the Saturday, I purposely took my walks round the Sally-
port, and the back of the Point (where hundreds of women
lived, and sailors resorted) to see their wickedness and misery,
that I might be the better able to point it out to them, which
I did this day, and told them I had seen it. I wept over them,
and felt more than I can express. I thought I could have
freely died for them, I loved their souls so well; but, ah!
there is one that has died for them. Oh, Christ, thou Son of
God! help them to see what thou hast done, and what thou
art still doing for them. It is the last time I may ever speak
to them again. Lord bless thy Word to their souls, that I
may meet some of them in glory!

"Wednesday, 5th August.—I arose tolerably early, considering my health. I feel this day (by reason of a cold) that I
can scarce speak to man; but, glory be to God, I can speak to
Him! I feel my soul much drawn out to God this day.—
Nothing but the fulness of God shall satisfy me. Oh, God!

my God! my portion, thou who art all my joy! come now and fill my soul, which, like a parched land, gasps for thee! Oh, that I were more glorious within! What riches, what fulness, do I see in my Jesus, who loads me daily with his favours From a sight and sense of my own unworthiness, I have thought this day, if ever I should reach heaven, I shall have the lowest place there, and be at every one's feet—a good and great place for a poor sinner; but I will aim for the highest p'ace; for there I shall, I doubt not, know more of God; but we shall all have enough to make us perfectly happy, or it would not be heaven. Lord! make me more holy here, and then I shall be more happy hereafter. I have this day been gasping on my bed with my asthmatic complaint. I could scarce get breath to draw; but, oh, my Jesus, my soul pants for thee! I have, blessed be God, got breath in my soul Jesus is all I want or desire In the evening I walked to a place called the Brick Kilns, where I preached from, 'So run that ye may obtain.' A good time it was to my soul. Oh, Lord, how great are thy mercies; make my faith and love greater!

"Thursday, 6th August.—My body seems a little better to day, but I dream and think much about mortality and death. I often, with a solemn joy, anticipate my departure I am patiently waiting the Lord's time, and waiting with joy to hear the rumbling of Christ's chariot-wheels. Come, O my Saviour, come! At the same time I am willing to live, if I am made useful, these forty years to come, for Christ is precious and souls are precious. I feel I have many temptations, but God is with me. I have many pleasing things offered to my view, but my will is lost in the will of God. O Lord, I am thirsting for more of thy divine fulness.

'Enlarge my heart to make thee room,
Enter, and ever in me stay'

"There is nothing that I love more than God I can give up all for Him; but still, Lord, do thou search me as with a candle, and if there be any wickedness in me, bid it all depart. My body, in the afternoon (owing to my asthmatic complaint) was very ill, so that I could scarcely breathe; but, Lord, I can breathe after Thee, and that is an unspeakable mercy. This afternoon I went to Horton Heath, where I preached, and a good time I had with the people of God."

His appointed term of service upon his circuit having expired, he returned home to his father's house at Wilton on the 7th August, 1795. In recording his return home, he says:

"I look back on the last year with a measure of sorrow and a great degree of shame that I have lived so little to God. I should, I doubt not, have been made far more useful had I lived nearer to Him; yet, blessed be His name, I have not spent my strength for nought, either as regards my own or others' souls. I reached home in the evening, and I prayed God in a particular manner to keep me from a deadness of soul, and to make me useful the few days I should spend with my friends."

It will be seen, from the foregoing extracts from his Diary, that he returned home much broken down in health: but he was too ardent in his Master's cause, and too much concerned for perishing souls, to remain idle. It appears from his Diary, that during the short time he sojourned with his family, though he needed rest, he continually preached in Wilton and the neighbouring towns, and spent much of his time in missionary labours amongst his fellow townsmen.

No sooner had he returned home, than the people on his circuit evinced their attachment to him by petitioning the Wesleyan Conference that he might be permitted to minister amongst them another year, and he was accordingly re-appointed; but before the appointment reached him, having received intelligence of what was going on, he began to look up for that direction without which he could not hope for any successful results from his renewed labours.

"I prayed much," he records, "that the Lord would not permit me to return were it not His will, and I believed I should not, if it were not so, and that, if I did return, I should be in my place."

His feelings, upon returning to his circuit, are thus expressed:

"Unfaithful as I was during the last year, and notwithstanding my unworthiness and very small abilities, the dear people of God received me with open arms O Lord, may I live nearer thee this year, that I may get more food for thy children."

CHAPTER V.

THE labours to which Mr. Crabb had now returned required a vigorous body and an untiring zeal. The former he did not possess, but the latter he did, in an eminent degree. Upon looking at the character of those labours, the privations and fatigues he had to endure, and the absence of any sordid temptation (for the remuneration he received was very small), we cannot but conclude that he acted under the influence of holy and heavenly motives. There was, no doubt—indeed he has acknowledged it — much of natural feeling and even vanity, mingled with what was spiritual and heavenly— but these were not the moving principles; they were the alloy in the precious metal, which the great Refiner ultimately, by the process through which He made him pass, " purged away." His Diary displays the true secret of his energy and diligence, his zeal and success. He lived " by his faith,"—faith was nourished by the word and strengthened by prayer, and prayer brought down into his soul, through the Spirit, continued supplies from the fulness of Him that filleth all in all.

Thus he went on his way rejoicing, finding the yoke of Christ easy and his burden light. He did not look for ease or comfort, and he was therefore not disappointed when hardship came upon him. He had counted the cost, and having put his hand to the plough, would not look back.

"I fully expected," he records, "many trials if I returned to my circuit, and I was not deceived ; but, glory be to God, I find strength according to my day, and—

'In all my temptations he has kept me to prove
His utmost salvation, his fulness of love.'

I realise, day by day, a greater sense of my own weakness in preaching and prayer ; but when I am weak, then am I strong, for I feel that the Lord is with me when I declare His truth. Lord, what am I that thou art mindful of me, who am less than the least of all thy mercies ? I have laboured much for many weeks in the Isle of Wight and in Portsmouth. In the latter place, I had several opportunities of preaching on the Point to the women and sailors. I think I may truly say, that people in general do not behave better in chapel than these people do here. May God Almighty have mercy upon many of them ! Many love me and always pay me due respect. If I chose, I might have plenty of money for preaching to them, but I quickly inform them that I don't preach for money I spent several hours in the middle of the day in going among them and conversing with them, sometimes in the corners of lanes, and sometimes in houses, and the Lord generally blesses his word. A poor sailor, a few days ago, came into the street and spoke to me, because he had seen me preaching I conversed with him about his soul, and assured him of the willingness of God to have mercy upon him. He wept, and three times affectionately shook hands with me. At different times, I met two women, who wept when I spoke to them. As many of these women are willing to leave their course of life, could they get anywhere to live, I think of setting a subscription on foot, for the purpose of getting them out of it. I have lately given them little books, many of which I have dropped about the streets, and I felt my soul much quickened in so doing. O! how I yearn over these precious souls.

"Nothing at present moves me, and blessed be God, I am enabled to live above everything I meet with. Lord, may I ever walk humbly, that I may walk safely! I have at this time two temptations peculiar to my nature. First, a temptation to pride; secondly, a temptation to please men in things by which I must certainly displease God, and in which, if I pleased men, I should not be the servant of Christ. Lord, make bare Thine arm in my behalf. Thou wilt keep those in perfect peace whose minds are stayed upon Thee."

But whilst he had many trials to endure, he had many mercies which more than counterbalanced them, and most, if not all, of which sprang from his trials. Of these he speaks in his Diary with peculiar delight; and as a few extracts from it may not be without profit, the following are presented to the reader:

"Tuesday, 6th September, 1795.—This is a sweet day to my soul—a day of watchfulness, a day of devotion, a day of humiliation before God. I am really ashamed that I make no more progress in the Divine life; but I desire to love my God more, and long to be swallowed up in Him. I have felt much this evening for precious souls, and have a great desire that God would bless my labours more; but I fear there is a great defect in me. I am not so holy as I ought to be. I do not (I am conscious) live the Gospel enough. I want to preach more out of the pulpit. I should do it, I know; and, by the help of God, I am this night determined to begin. Lord, help me! I have determined this evening to read the Scriptures more, and to live them more. O Lord, let thy Spirit enlighten me when I read, that in speaking of thy word I may ever bring out of the Treasury things new and old appertaining to the kingdom. I can say, of a truth, that in reading the word of God, my soul is blessed and my heart often warmed. O for more of this ! Quicken my soul, O Lord, and make me truly alive to thee, and give me such a measure of thy presence that I may always be in the Spirit, always ready for Thy will. Amen. Amen.

"Monday, 21st.—This was a sweet day to my soul ; retirement was sweet, the Scriptures were sweet, and meditation was sweet, and, above all, Jesus was sweet. I sank this day, as in many past days—from a deep sense of my unworthiness and weakness—low at the feet of Christ. I saw myself fit for nothing, nor worthy of anything ; but Christ was all in all to my soul. I was this day very sensible of the importance of the work of the ministry, and having this evening to preach in Newport, I almost sank under a sense of my weakness, unworthiness, and inability ; but glory be to God, I can say, that whilst I was holding forth the words of eternal life, my whole soul was so swallowed up in God, that I seemed to dwell in heaven. O my God, how sweet are the visits of thy grace to my soul ! This evening, in private, I was a prevailing Jacob. I had from God, my Father, whatever my heart desired.

"Thursday, 24th.—I walked from Nethercomb to Godshill. On the road I had many pleasing temptations and baits offered to me ; but through all, my soul was kept looking unto Jesus. My eye of faith discerned not only the bait, but the hook ; not only the pleasure, but the poison.* Good Lord, still deliver me ! I retired all day to my chamber (having no people to visit), and it was truly a profitable day to my soul. I gained more light in the Scriptures than I had for many days before ; and I not only got more light, but I obtained more warmth and vigour of soul. Lord, what am I, that thou art mindful of me ? I was afraid, however, that this day I did not sufficiently feel a sense of my unworthiness, and this led me to pray that the Lord would, by some means (I was indifferent what means they were), humble my soul still deeper than ever. My God

---

* It is the remark of Plato, that if our pleasures looked upon us when they came to us, as they do when they turn their backs upon us, we should never entertain them. Happy he who, by Divine grace, sees in them the end from the beginning, or, as Mr. Crabb expresses it, "not only the bait, but the hook !"

heard me, and to His name be the glory ; my soul was humbled, so that I was enabled to cry out :

> ' O ! for a closer walk with God,
> A calm and heavenly frame ;
> A light to shine upon the road,
> That leads me to the Lamb.'

" Wednesday, 21st October, 1795.—I arose with this prayer, Lord, keep me all this day by thy grace. I did not this morning feel much power in prayer ; but my soul leaned on Jesu's bosom. I felt a steady and settled peace in my God, and my determination was to live nearer to Him than ever. Towards the middle of the day I set out for Freshwater. It was very wet and dirty all the way, and I was soon wet through. My boots and umbrella being almost worn out, made it disagreeable to flesh and blood. Though it was but a little way from Yarmouth to Freshwater, yet with the wind, rain, dirt, and want of food, I was so worn out with weakness, that I was obliged to take rest by leaning against a gate. I searched the almost barren hedges for provision, and when I could find any it was very acceptable. O Lord, may I gather fruit from thee continually ! My soul at this time much rejoiced in God, and indeed in winds and storms He is a sweet portion to my soul. O that I had more of His image !

" Friday, 23rd October.—This day, going from one place to another, I walked nearly twenty miles. This evening my missionary labours ended for a few days, and I returned home with a cheerful heart, for my days, especially the week past, have been crowned with mercies, though I have not been without my crosses. I have been wet through every day since I set off, have not tasted a bit of meat since Tuesday, and sometimes hedge fruit was a substitute for everything. Lord, what a mercy I could get this ! O that my heart was more thankful ! I find it good to mortify my body ; it brings my spirit into subjection. I was at the prayer-meeting this evening, after I got home ; it was a profitable, humbling season to my soul. I saw my short comings to a great degree. I was afterwards employed in reading ; but my body began to want rest, though I almost grudged the time for it. O that I bound up every moment for God ! I thought

it was almost a pity that my poor body wanted so much rest.
What a mercy that all labour and toil will be over in heaven.
O Lord, prepare me for that rest ! After I got into bed, I had
one of the best times I have had for a great while ; I seemed as
one in heaven, and all my heart was praise. Oh ! my Father,
I'll praise thee better by and bye !

"30th November, 1795—I this day went from Cowes to
Newport, and from Newport to Youngwoods, to see my brother
Etheridge. Passing over the forest I lost myself, but I was
enabled to cast my care upon the Lord. After tea, I walked off
for Shefflett, where I preached My road all the way from
Newport was like a river, and I was generally half a leg high
in water and dirt I could bless the Lord that I was counted
worthy to bear these little crosses, and I had a present reward
in them. I preached after I got to the house, though I was
very wet I had a good time with the people, and I know the
Lord was in our midst After preaching, I had three miles to
walk, and through water almost all the way. On the road I
was so fatigued with walking, preaching, and want of food, that
I could hardly stand : once I fell down with weakness O my
God, it is good to bear a little for thee ; I am not worthy thus to
be honoured ! After a little refreshment, I recovered strength
and retired to bed. I found afterwards Christ very precious to
my soul, and I was much drawn out unto God in prayer and
thanksgiving.

" Wednesday, 2nd December, 1795.—I arose with a body
somewhat impaired ; but, blessed be God, I am not weary of the
work to which the Lord hath called me. At about nine o'clock
I set off for Newport. I had to walk through wet and dirt, as
usual, half a leg high, and sometimes higher ; but I thought on
the road I would not change my state with any person in
England I found my heart engaged in the good work, and
the more labour the more grace I wanted ; therefore all was,
through grace, welcome to me I called on brother Etheridge
on the road, where I dined. As I was walking across the forest,
in the evening, I was sensibly convinced that I had not improved
my time at brother Etheridge's, as I ought to have done, by
good and spiritual conversation. I was sorry for it, and could
not help kneeling down in the West Forest to ask my Father's

pardon. O what a grief it is to me that my words are not always seasoned with grace : Lord, forgive the sin of thy servant, and help me to be more watchful for the time to come ! This evening I felt myself quite ill, not having had any dry boots for three days ; but my dear Lord satisfies me with His grace.

"9th December.—I this day set off for Portsmouth. We had a great many passengers on board, and many of them were the wives of soldiers, who had embarked for the West Indies. We had a distressing scene on board. About one o'clock a very heavy gale of wind came on, with hail, rain, thunder and lightning. The captain saw it coming, and ordered every sail to be taken down, so that we were then at the mercy of the waves, though I knew they had a Master. The vessel rolled and tossed terrifically. Many were sick, some crying, and most fearing. I felt myself in a very composed frame of mind. I found I had nothing to do but to cast my care on Jesus, and to embrace the waves if His will. We were in a sad predicament, having so many women and children on board, so for near an hour I turned nurse to a noisy child, whose mother was very ill. Previous to this I had a very searching time to my own soul. I saw my short comings to a great degree, and was ashamed and confounded before God ; nevertheless I found I was in a measure growing in grace. Bless the Lord, O my soul ! A little after two in the afternoon, I was landed in Portsmouth, and though there had been much loss of life and of many vessels during the gale, yet the unworthiest on this side of hell was preserved. Lord, I trust it is for a good purpose ! The people in Portsmouth were glad to see me, though I wondered why they loved me.

"14th December, 1795.—I did not rise very early this morning, being almost worn out, and when I did rise I was full of pain. My side" (in which he had continual pain) "got still worse, so that it was with difficulty at times I could get my hand to my head. My appetite in a great measure fails from inward fever, and my spirits sink ; but, blessed be the God of my salvation, I feel my heart lifted towards my eternal home : every pain brings fresh comfort, for it bears with it fresh news from the Courts above. I am now only waiting for my change, saying, ' Father, not as I will, but as thou wilt.' O, it is good to suffer for Jesus !

Did I say suffer? I can hardly call it suffering, for my best moments are when in pain, and even then labour is more welcome than rest. Though I am so poorly, I am now preparing to walk six or seven miles through wet and dirt; though I cannot apparently walk a mile, I cannot give up the work for one day: I cannot miss one congregation. My heart would, as it were, bleed for them. O sweet labour, welcome to my poor unworthy soul! O what a sabbath shall I by-and-bye have with those children whom the Lord now and then has given me! Just as I was setting off, the Lord by his providence mercifully sent me a horse. O how well to be in a way of duty! I set off immediately. Before I got half my journey over I was much tired: my heart beat excessively, and my fever increased; but, blessed be God, my love for souls also increased. About six my congregation came, and they were now double to what I had last time; and very much affected they seemed to be. Many of them, as far as in their power, manifest a great love for me. I had a good time with them, and was well paid for my trouble and pain. Lord, make thy word to them as nails fastened in a sure place, never more to be removed! After preaching I rode three miles to get a bed, as it was not convenient for me to sleep in Shefflett. I find it better to ride than walk through water and dirt.

"Saturday, 19th December, 1795.—I could hardly this day get out of my bed, the pain in my side was so much augmented; I seem getting nearer and nearer to my eternal rest. My anchor is within the veil; but I am this morning constrained to cry out, 'My unfaithfulness! my unworthiness!' I believe I shall by-and-bye pass through death's shadow with great triumph, though not without blushing and shamefacedness. O thou eternal Beam, thou Sun of Righteousness, why art thou not withdrawn from such a wretch as I am? Oh! ye blessed angels of light, ye ministering spirits, why are ye attendant on such a worm as I? I see the reason—Jesus loves and intercedes for me; His father hears and loves me. 'Amazing love! how can it be, that thou, O my God, shouldst think of me?' But it is by grace I am saved, and what a mercy not by works of righteousness.

"Sunday, 20th.—I rose this morning early, though the

pain in my side was not much, if any, abated. My spirits were
pretty good, so that I could the better bear up under my little
suffering. Between seven and eight o'clock I set out to preach
at East Cowes, though I was quite unfit; but I was willing to
try. I was two hours walking the five miles. It is good to
crawl in the way of duty, if I cannot run. At half-past ten I
preached to a small congregation, and had a very gracious time
with them. The Lord blessed me of a truth, and, by what I
could see and hear, the people felt the power of God's word.
In the afternoon I heard the Rev. Mr. Walker preach, and in
the evening I preached in his pulpit. We had a tolerable congregation, and a very gracious time. I could hardly stand
through weakness. I was so weak that I thought I should
have fallen down. I preached from, 'The wages of sin is
death.' O may it prove the savour of life unto life, and not of
death unto death. After preaching in the evening, I rode from
Cowes to Newport. I went to rest much fatigued with the
labour of the day. Lord, I would bless thee for that mercy
which thou hast shown me this day.

"Monday, 21st.—I seem a little better in body, though, as I
have observed, my disorder is of a flattering nature. It having
been proposed that I should go home for a week or ten days
for advice and for a little rest, I have written for a preacher
to come and supply my place ; otherwise I could not be easy in
going home. In the morning I set out for Shefflett, where I
preached in the evening. I had not many, the weather being
very wet. I had a good time with the people, and the Lord
was with us. After I had preached I had three miles to go in
the rain and wind; but I felt a willingness this evening to
die in the cause of God, labouring for the good of souls. Lord,
I am in thy hands : do with me as seemeth good unto Thee.

"Thursday, 24th December, 1795.—At six in the morning
I took coach, and set off home (twenty-five miles), and at the
end of my journey was completely laid up. Lord, what a
shattered tenement do I carry about with me. I bless God
that my soul is in any measure healthy. At family prayer this
evening we all had an astonishing time ; the power of God was
felt much, and we could not help weeping for joy, especially
my greyheaded father.

' Praise God from whom all blessings flow.' "

In the course of Mr. Crabb's visitations amongst the poor on his circuit, and those of his native town, he often met with many who languished from sickness and disease whom he had no power to relieve. Touched by their sufferings, he determined to associate the healing of the sick with the preaching of the Gospel, and he was especially led to this by the example of our Lord, who not only went about teaching, but healing " all manner of sickness and all manner of disease" among the people, and who, when He sent forth the seventy, directed them to heal the sick. He saw, moreover, that our Lord, not only during His ministry on earth, but after his ascension, conferred miraculous gifts upon those who preached, or were engaged in making known the Gospel, to enable them to cure disease; and he inferred from all this that these gifts were bestowed, not merely to prove the Divine origin of Christianity, but as a means to its reception by those who were the subjects of, or witnessed the cures which were effected. Knowing that the heart of man is still as hard, and its natural enmity still as great, as it was in Apostolic days, and that God now uses means and human instrumentalities where before he wrought miracles, Mr. Crabb immediately applied himself to the acquisition of such a degree of medical knowledge as might be useful. Having purchased a few medical books he obtained some acquaintance with the properties of various drugs and their application to the cure of particular diseases, and he acquired from a few pious medical friends some practical knowledge which he found useful, both in the management of his own health and the treatment of those who became his "patients." It appears, from entries in his Diary between the years 1795 and 1798, that he spent some time almost every week in compounding medicines for the sick, and that he rarely visited where he was likely to meet with cases of sickness without being furnished with drugs that might be useful. Some of the cures he effected, and which he has recorded in his Journal, seem almost incredible; and I am told that his treatment of cases of ague, which abounded in the marshy places on his circuit, was so successful, that his skill was known and talked of by the people far and near.

These medical attempts tended greatly to the furtherance of the Gospel, for though Mr. Crabb's kindness of manner generally obtained for him admission to most places, yet no sooner was it known that he possessed some skill in medicine than he found an open door in places where before he had no access; and he was thus able, not only to relieve the bodily sufferings of those whom he visited, but to bring "nigh unto them the kingdom of God;" for whenever he administered medicine he invariably prayed with the individual for a blessing; and he so prayed as to impress upon those who were present the solemn realities of eternity; and whenever relief was afforded, it gave weight to what he said, and enabled him to be more bold and earnest in bringing before them the important topics of the disease of the soul—Christ the physician—the judgments of God against sin—His mercy in Christ, and the efficacy of prayer—topics which, when the heart was softened by a sense of mercy received, often struck home to the conscience, and in many instances led to conversion.

The practical importance of associating the healing art with the promulgation of the Gospel is now beginning to be felt, especially with reference to missions to the heathen; and I doubt not it will be found that one great reason why our Christian missions have answered our

expectations so little, is, that this most important concomitant of missionary work has been lost sight of. Souls
are precious; and as the church of God cannot afford to
lose any appliance, however feeble, that opens the way for
the Christian Missionary, it will be well to consider whether
what Heaven has in mercy joined together should any
longer be kept asunder. We read that two angels—
though one doubtless might have sufficed—were sent to
rescue Lot, and that "whilst he lingered *they* laid hold
upon his hand, and upon the hands of his wife, and upon
the hand of his two daughters; the Lord being merciful unto
him; and they brought him forth and set him without
the city:"—and thus may it often be that medicine, sent
forth as the companion of the Gospel, may help to lay
hold upon the hand of those who tarry in the place of
destruction and bring them to one of safety!*

* The importance of connecting the art of medicine with
the preaching of the Gospel has of late years been brought to
the notice of the principal Missionary Societies in Europe; and
there is now scarcely a mission to the heathen in which one
missionary, at least, is not possessed of some knowledge of
medicine and surgery. In such a mission as that to China,
the missionary who understands the cure of disease, especially of
ophthalmia (so prevalent there), will find access to families, villages, towns and cities where, without such a qualification, he
would not be permitted to enter, and it is notorious, that where
the heathen, whether in China, or elsewhere, are benefited by
the medical skill of those who come to them, they are often, like
Naaman, led to say, "Behold, now I know that there is no God
in all the earth but in Israel; thy servant will henceforth offer
neither burnt offering nor sacrifice unto other gods, but unto the
Lord." The Chinese Evangelization Society has lately been established in London upon these combined principles, and past
experience justifies the expectation that abundant success will,
under the blessing of the Most High, attend its efforts amongst
the idolatrous myriads of that empire.

Mr. Crabb had now returned home to his father's house at Wilton, his astonishing labours having brought him nearly to the brink of the grave; but, reduced as he was, he could not remain inactive, as the entry in his Diary, on the day after his arrival home, will show:

"Friday, 25th December.—In the morning I heard the Rev. Mr. Edwards (the Dissenting Minister) preach in Wilton, and was much blessed under the word. In the afternoon I preached in Salisbury, as poor brother McKenzie was worse than myself. What a mercy it is to be in church fellowship, and that we can be helps one to another. I had a good time with the people. Lord, may thy people take warning, and not neglect thy great salvation. Being almost laid up by the time I had finished my day's work, I applied to an apothecary for advice, who informed me that my debility was brought on by too much fatigue, and that there was danger of consumption. I was now regular in my diet, lived chiefly on soups, rode out every day, and took bracing and stomachic medicine two and three times a day. What a mercy the Lord hath given unto man wisdom in any measure to be useful to his fellow man. I was at home nearly one month, and I have reason to bless God for it; for, first, my body is better; second, there has been a blessed revival in my own family; and, third, more of the spirit of Christ appears among God's children, for I have been allowed to preach for Mr. Edwards (a Baptist Minister) nine times, to astonishing numbers of people, with whom I had good times; and from the testimony of many, I believe bigotry is, in a great measure, laid aside, and they have more love for the despised people called Methodists. I did nothing but preach Christ to them, and many were surprised, for they thought we always preached a covenant of works. Thou, Lord, shalt have glory for this."

In the course of a few weeks his health became so far re-established that on the 21st January, 1796, he was able to return to his circuit:

"I took," he records, "a horse, as my doctor assures me I must walk no more for the present. The day I set out I was obliged to ride twenty-five miles, from home to Southampton, and when I arrived the people made me preach."

From an entry made ten days after this in his Diary, it was evident that his health was again giving way :

"My trials," he writes, "increase, and I am in heaviness. Oh, what a needs be there is for them. Time shall discover this in part, but eternity shall reveal it fully. Oh, blessed day ! I shall soon behold it. I was, through mercy, enabled to bear all with a degree of patience, so that in the fire I did not melt into peevishness, but into humility and love. Oh, Spirit of God ! Thou art my Sanctifier ; and Thou shalt have all the glory. I walked this day to Arreton, about three miles ; but I find my body will not bear it. I preached there, and had a glorious time. I had to walk from Arreton about a mile, to get a bed, and by the time I got there I was completely laid up. Lord ! what a poor, weak, and useless creature I am about to be ; but, oh ! make use of me in some way or other. I am Thine, do with me as Thou wilt."

On Saturday, the 5th February, 1796, he was suddenly called from Portsmouth, where he was labouring, to South-ampton, to occupy on the Sabbath the post of a brother-labourer, who was incapable of further work. He appears to have walked the whole distance, eighteen miles ; but such was his state of debility, that the journey occupied the whole day. In noticing this circumstance in his Journal he writes,—"Lord, I had rather die in than out of harness :"

' O for a trumpet voice, on all the world to call,' &c.

I had the mercy of God for my portion all the day. Oh blessed portion !"

On the Sabbath he could scarcely walk to and from the chapel ; but he preached three times, and records that he

had gracious seasons. After this he preached at Timsbury, Houghton, Whitchurch, Ryde, and Southampton.
He reached the last-mentioned place on Sunday, the 13th
February, and after preaching in the morning, and resting
in bed till the afternoon, he was enabled to preach in the
evening:

"When I began," he records, "I could scarcely stand or
kneel in the pulpit; but whilst I was engaged in the glorious
work, I was strengthened in body and soul, so that I left off
better than I began. The night of this Sabbath, however, was
one of much pain and suffering, and death appeared to be near
in prospect."

He records that, like David, he watered his couch with
his tears:

"I began," he says, "to look back upon my Christian course,
and saw that my life filled up with nothing but unfaithfulness.
Shame took hold upon me. I was confounded before God.
My cry was, Lord what have I been doing? I have been as a
dwarf in thy vineyard, when I ought to have been as a cedar
in Lebanon. I am determined this day to set out afresh.
Lord, help me by thy Spirit. I have reason to bless God;
for in the midst of all my tears I have a hope full of immortality. My anchor is cast within the veil, and I shall soon be
where hope shall be turned into joy."

Notwithstanding the state of his health, he still persisted
in labouring. On the 25th of the same month, there is
this entry in his Diary:

"This is Passion day. It is a solemn season to my soul.
Oh, that I always set the Lord before me as I do now, and
Jesus would be more precious. How can *I* doubt the mercy of
God? I *know* my heavenly Father loves me, and will be
always with me. In the evening I had to preach in Salisbury;
I had about an hour for retirement, and, blessed be God, it
was not altogether spent in vain. If ever I was in an agony
of soul, it was this evening. In prayer I seemed to have firm
hold on the horns of the altar. I grasped Christ in his per-

fections and promises with more fervency that ever. My body was quite overcome through the wrestling power I had with God."

Again; on Wednesday, the 30th March, he writes:

"As a prince, I have power with God this day. He is, I know, deepening His work in my soul. Oh, my Jesus work in me for Thine own glory, and fill me with Thyself! I have been for a long time past (indeed, ever since I have been ill) impressed with the duty of giving up travelling (itinerating), as my apothecary, who is a zealous and godly man, tells me I never shall be able to travel as I have done. At other times, I have had some impression to fix in a congregation, and to the end that I may be able to do so, I have thought (it having been represented to me to be necessary) of going to an academy to study divinity, and get some knowledge of languages. At other times, I have had impressions to stay at home with my father, and take part in his business, and be a supernumerary preacher; but I am standing still to see the salvation of God. I am willing to be anything so that I may but please Christ, and He knows this. I have been continually in prayer about these things, but particularly this day; and after much time spent in that exercise and in examination, it seems to me that I ought to desist from travelling; but I am not clearly convinced of this, and must, therefore, still wait upon God. Glory be to my heavenly Father, I am willing to suffer affliction with the people of God. Oh, may I seek the glory of God, and not mine own ease, honour, pleasure, or any thing like it. There is nothing in my heart that I cannot gladly give up for the Lord. I would not live for earth. I am more nobly born. I would hate the thought of being my own director. Lord, thou art the potter, and I am the clay. Do with me as thou wilt!"

He was now compelled to return home to recruit his strength. During the time he remained at Wilton, he employed himself in the diligent study of the Word, and in prayer and attendance on the means of grace. He prescribed medicine for the poor, and sometimes he

preached. Having a good constitution, he soon felt the
benefit of rest, and the symptoms of disease which had
appeared having abated, and his health become partially
restored, he panted to return to the scene of his former
labours. It was clear, however, that he could no longer
endure the fatigues of his former circuit, and therefore he
was appointed to that of Salisbury, on which the journeys
were not so great, and in which he had the advantage of
being, in case he should again break down, nearer to his
home. His father having provided him with a horse for
travelling, he set off from home on the 16th September,
1796, on which occasion he took a stock of drugs for the
use of the sick who might be thrown in his way. The
entries in his Diary during the time he laboured in this
new sphere are of a deeply spiritual character, and whilst
they display an uninterrupted intercourse with heaven,
exhibit its never-failing concomitant, a gradual growth in
grace. That his zeal in the service of his Divine Master
was unabated, and that his consolations from above were
unfailing, will be seen from the following entry in his
Diary, under the date of Sunday, the 30th December,
1796:

" I rose this morning early ; had much confidence and liberty
in prayer. In the morning, I preached from 1 John ii. 13, 14.
The text was given me whilst I was in the pulpit My
thoughts were new, and all immediately given me of God. I
find it is better to depend on God, and get my matter from
him, the pure fountain. I never had such a time in my life.
My soul seemed to border on the celestial land ; yea, sometimes,
it seemed as though I stepped into it. O God, do not suffer me
to trust in any arm but thine. The favour and presence of
Jehovah were so realised by me, that it shook my poor tabernacle almost to pieces, and it was with much pain I reached
Shaftesbury about one o'clock In the afternoon I preached

from Isaiah xxvi. 20, 21. I had a very gracious time. I was tempted to leave my simplicity at the bottom of the pulpit-stairs, but, blessed be God, I took it up into the pulpit with me, and experienced that my sufficiency was of God. Lord, let Thy word be as bread cast on the waters. At half-past five, I had to preach at our own chapel. The chapel was so full that I could scarcely get in, and before we had done singing the people were as thick as bees; the very aisles being crammed full. The walls and pulpit and my clothes were wet with the breath of the people. I was much affected at the sight, and was so weak when I began that I could scarcely speak; but I began in the strength of the Lord, and did not begin in vain. I had much of my Master's presence, and the people were much affected, whilst my soul was filled with love towards them. By the time I had finished my sermon, I could hardly stand or speak; but, Lord, it is a good, yea, the best cause to die in. After preaching I met the society, and gave them an exhorta-tion. I closed the day with a happy soul, but a worn-out body. I felt much of the favour of Jesus on my bed, after I retired for the night."

It appears that he was much disappointed at what he saw on this circuit; and upon a review of his labours, he says:

"My spirits were much cast down to see at what a low ebb the Gospel was. Lord, whence is it? I have now gone round the Salisbury Circuit, and my grief is, that I have not found more genuine piety among the people. O Lord, I want to see all Thy people striving for sanctification, and to be wholly con-formed to Thee! What is religion without that?"

He returned from his circuit in January, 1797, but no sooner had he reached home than his services were again required; his companion in the Gospel, who was to suc-ceed him, having broken down, and being wholly unable to labour. This was no unusual thing in those days, in which the labourers were so few, that they were obliged to travel from place to place, even on the Sabbath. So

great were the fatigues and privations of these men of God
—as may be seen from Mr. Crabb's Diary—that many of
them sank under them.   There is scarcely a burial-place
throughout the districts where they laboured, that does
not contain the remains of some of those devoted men.
Their very names are now almost forgotten upon earth;
and no wonder; for they preached to the poor and the
neglected, to the houseless wanderer and the deserted out-
cast—to those for whose souls no other men cared, and to
whom no other men preached; and there is no *éclat,*
nothing dazzling in that.   Pride would not stoop to look
upon them, gentility scorned them, and apostolical succession denounced them as deceivers and impostors; but
"their names are written in heaven—their record is on
high."   They were the ambassadors of Christ, and He
sealed their labours by His Spirit; and on that day—

> " When the Archangel's blast
> Shall winnow, like a fan, the chaff and grain,"

they shall be His, for whom they "counted their lives not
dear unto them : " He "shall dwell among them; they
shall hunger no more, neither thirst any more ; the days
of their mourning shall be ended, and God shall wipe all
tears from their eyes."

> "Oh! blest are they who live and die like these."

How Mr. Crabb survived his astonishing labours and
sufferings is marvellous ; but " God's servants are immortal
till their work is done."

Mr. Crabb having, under the circumstances already
referred to, been required to return to his circuit, immediately obeyed.   His renewed labours, however, were much too
great for him, and it appears from his Diary that he was
often on the point of breaking down : but he still went

on, supported by the strength which is perfected in weakness.

Amongst many entries in his Diary at this period I find the following, which may not be unprofitable to the young minister :

"Sunday, 6th January, 1797.—I preached in the morning at Notcomb, to a good congregation. There was, I found, a person amongst them who was a judge of sermons, and I was tempted to alter my text ; but I prayed that I might cease to exist that moment, rather than aim to please man. I was to change my text, because I had not studied it much ! but blessed be God, I was delivered, and God was with me. I do not know when I had a better time, and a great many new thoughts were given me in preaching, that perhaps I should never have received had I studied an hour. In the afternoon I preached in Shaftesbury. I had a very dead time indeed ; but a great part of my deadness was owing to my body. I was very weak and full of pain in my breast, and so I continued till I began to preach in the evening ; and then, as Whitefield used to say, the pulpit-sweat cured me. I had 1,000 persons to preach to, and attentive they were. My fever was very strong in the night, but blessed be God for the flames of his love in my heart !"

How much he relied for success on the prayers of the Lord's people, the want of which is so often the reason of a dead and profitless ministry, will be seen from what he has himself recorded :

"Wednesday, 9th January.—I rode to Stalbridge. O my dear Father, how deplorable is this place ! I could hardly get a word out of my mouth in preaching or in prayer. Lord, I fear there are no praying people here. I know not that I ever had such a time. Some people's religion seems to consist in finding fault with others. Lord, help me to esteem others better than myself ! This is the spirit of the Gospel.

"5th February.—I could not help weeping this evening, under a sense of the goodness, mercy, and love of God towards me.

O my God, when shall I love Thee more ! Blessed be thy name, I feel momentarily a nearness towards Thee. O how sweet is the love of God ! My soul this night, yea till midnight, was lost in prayer for my brother and family. I believe God will hear me in my every petition."

How much he lived above the things of time, could rejoice in circumstances in which most men would be sorrowful, and how little he considered himself when he could benefit his fellow men, will be seen from the following passages, taken from his Diary:

"7th February, 1797.—I walked to Salisbury with my father, and had a profitable conversation. Being in so large a way of business, he is suffering irreparable losses, and owing to the present war trade is getting so dead, that instead of keeping 500 hands, it is probable he will not keep more than 252 ; but, blessed be God, I never saw him supported under trials as he is now. I am sure he has the grace of God. Bless the Lord, O my soul, and forget not this great mercy ! The whole of my afternoon was taken up in seeking after hemlock for a poor woman who has the king's evil. I got wet in my feet, and hence a bad cold ; but I am willing to suffer anything for the good of my fellow-creatures, in body or soul.

" 9th March, 1797.—In the morning, after commending my body and soul by prayer in faith to the keeper of Israel, I set off for Wilton on foot, which is nineteen miles distant. Many of the people were rather hurt at my walking, because they knew I did not want for money, as I had so kind a father ; but I could not in conscience give away a half-crown to ride when I thought I could walk, and I knew the half-crown would help the poor peasants as I walked along, and open a way for me to say something to them about their souls ; and I found on the road my end was answered. 'Tis often a grief to me when I consider I have spent so many pounds in superfluities both before and after conversion, and I consider I must soon give an account of every farthing I spend. God be merciful unto me, and pardon the sins of my youth, and help me to be watchful for the future. Good Lord ! how many more bellies might I have filled, and how many more backs might I have clothed! Thou knowest, Lord, my determination is henceforth to live to thy glory, and give all my money as well as my time, my talents, &c., to Thee. Lord, help a worm by thy good Spirit! I longed for my closet as soon as I reached home. O how sweet is prayer!"

The instance of self-denial, recorded in the extract above given, is not a solitary one, for I find in his Diaries many similar instances, some of which were imprudent, inasmuch as he wore out his strength by excessive fatigue, and thus incapacitated himself for duty. But these things show the character of the man. In this matter few err as he did; and when the principle which actuated him is regarded, who would not rather have made his mistakes than those which many of the Lord's people make? Surely he had much of the Spirit of Him, who though rich, for our sakes became poor, that we through His poverty might be rich. Thus acting and thus living, he inherited a blessing from on high, and can we, therefore, wonder when we read the following:

"15th March, 1797.—I know not when I was ever so happy as I am this night; I seem to be caught up—I can hardly tell where. O Christ, how precious art thou to my soul! I live now as on the borders of heaven. I often catch a glance of it by faith. O happy place, for my God is there! I live now every moment in God, and He dwells in me. I have trying moments, but no dark ones. I have tempting moments, but find God keeps me, 1 Peter, i. 5; Heb. vii. 25. By a life of faith in the Son of God, I find his blood thoroughly washes me every moment, so that I know, through that alone, I stand whole, and have a full and constant salvation. O unworthy sinner! O helpless worm! Dear Jesus, I come and lie at thy feet—a place infinitely too high for me."

After continuing some time longer on his circuit, he returned home, where he remained to recruit his health; but

It being apparent that he was no longer able to endure the fatigues of itinerancy, under the advice of his friends, he resigned his office. The two extracts which follow, from his Diary, will show the "manner of life" he now led, and the schemes of usefulness in which he employed himself:

"Thursday, 7th September, 1797.—I arose early, and after much prayer, I set off for my morning's ride on the sea-shore before breakfast. The Lord was with me. Between seven and eight I returned, and went to my closet for near an hour. God was very present with me, and satisfied my soul abundantly We had good and profitable conversation at breakfast, and I had much of God (though much tempted) in family prayer. After breakfast I retired to my closet for some time, and found it good to be there In the evening, having to preach, I retired to my closet, where I had sweet promises and much of God in prayer, and believed that He would help me. It was according to my faith. O how did God set my soul at liberty! I had a praying and believing soul, and much of the presence of my Master. The people were much blessed, and God helped them to believe I plainly see that for a preacher to be great and precious in the sight of God, and to be useful to the people, he must be simple and sincere, aiming at people's souls, and not to be fine or eloquent It is not our oratory that makes us useful It may gratify our pride and delight itching ears; but it will not bring souls to Christ. We want piety and simplicity. We may sink into hell with our gifts, but we cannot with the grace of God in our hearts. O how sad is it when ministers strive for the applause of their congregation, or preach to please themselves. O my God! my God, I have thus been guilty; but through thy grace I have repented, and trust I am reformed When I lost my simplicity, how little was my love for souls,— how careful to please myself and gain the attention of man. O how I am ashamed of this before God! Perhaps some poor souls went to hell through my fine (or rather want of plainer) preaching. O I could weep, as it were, tears of blood, on account of this ! Blessed be God, I am now delivered. I am now, I believe, only aiming at souls, and I don't care by what means or language I can get them out of the hands of Satan. Lord, keep me simple!

"Friday, 8th.—I was so fatigued that I did not rise early. Private and family prayer were sweet to my poor soul. I know I love the Lord. After breakfast I retired to my closet for a great part of the morning, and the blessings I there obtained from my God can never be described by pen or tongue. I meet my God everywhere and in every thing, especially in my closet. I had more direction this day in my closet than I have had for months past, though God's way is quite contrary to mine. In much mercy he removed all my objections in one minute, and made me willing to love his way. O how sweetly and softly does the Spirit of God administer grace, and yet how powerfully! In the afternoon traps were laid for my soul by the devil; but my God delivered me, and will deliver me. The employment of the closet was this evening so sweet, that I could not venture into my bed till between eleven and twelve. I mourn my ingratitude and littleness of love before God. O that this heart were more fired with love, and more earnestly employed for God.

CHAPTER VI.

Preaches in his Native Town.—Diary.—His Acquaintance with
Miss Raddon. — His Letter to her, offering Marriage. — His
Marriage.—Reflections.

THE discoveries which Mr. Crabb made in the course of his
visitations amongst the people of Wilton, of their gross
ignorance and depravity, led him to the determination of
making some effort to disseminate the Gospel amongst
them.   To this end, he hired a room in the house of one
of his father's workmen, and having obtained a license, he
opened it as a Dissenting place of worship.   This circumstance and its results, and the other schemes of usefulness
in which at this time he engaged, will best appear from
what he has himself recorded :

" 3rd November, 1797.—This day I engaged with one of our
foremen to have his house to preach in, for, by the help of God,
I and the travelling preachers are determined to lift up the
standard of Christ against sin, and for the salvation of souls.
O God, bless us in our attempt !   Blessed be God, he hath now
heard and answered prayer.   How long have I been praying for this day !   I have been much taken up of late, to get
some pious people from different parts to work for us, that they
may be helpful in carrying on prayer-meetings, and now God
hath exceeded my expectations.

" Sunday, 5th November.—I arose this morning before light,
and found my mind suitably and seriously impressed.   I have

set apart this day for abstinence and prayer. Blessed be the Lord ! I feel my mind truly serious. I do believe God is about to do something great for me O God, prepare me for it ! Amen and amen. At nine o'clock, I retired for an hour's prayer. I had a solemn time of it In the morning I went to the meeting, and heard the Rev Mr War'ow. I had a very seasonable and profitable time, God was with us indeed. At one o'clock, I retired to my closet, and set apart the whole after-noon for prayer, as I intend, with the Lord's help, to deliver the whole counsel of God to my fellow-Wilton sinners. I remained in my closet till between four and five o'clock. I felt much liberty in prayer for Wilton. I do believe God will do something great for it. At tea, God's presence was with me, and He humbled my soul. After tea, I retired to my closet, and was there in prayer for an hour before preaching-time, and God was with me. When I got to the newly-licensed house, it was so full, even for yards outside the doors, that I found it difficult to get in, and many were obliged to go away. O what a night is this ! I had power from on high while preaching to them, and I believe they felt it very powerfully. O Lord, let not thy word fall to the ground ! I was so very earnest for poor souls, through the rich grace of God towards me, that I was quite exhausted. My fever was very high after preaching; but, O my God ! what a good cause to be exhausted in. Let me praise Thee with my latest breath O my soul, never forget the fifth of November, 1797 ! May Wilton never forget it ! O my God, let it be the beginning of good days ! I ended the day in my closet, between ten and eleven o'clock

"Monday, 6th November.—I could not rise before six this morning. In the hours of devotion I felt and enjoyed fresh light, and my soul dwelt in the presence of God all the day. I was engaged in Salisbury and Wilton, to get seats and a pul-pit for our new place of worship. O my God, be thou seated amongst us in mercy and love ! I had but little time for closet-duty ; but God, even my God, made it up to me, for I had a sweet sense of His presence and approbation. As I had so little time for closet-duty this day, I was desirous of making it up in the evening, I remained up till between eleven and twelve, reading, praying, &c, and I found it profitable.

"Tuesday, 21st November. — I awoke this morning, between two and three o'clock, with a burning fever, but the moment I awoke my soul was all prayer and praise. I could not help rising immediately to pray unto Him for myself and others, and one in particular (this was Miss Martha Raddon, his future wife), who was upon my mind. I slept no more after this, for I was very ill. O my God! what a mercy I have peace with Thee in affliction, and a hope full of immortality! All the morning, I found my mind stayed upon God, though I was very weak in my body. O God, while I live, let it be to thee!

*   *   *   *   *   *   *

"I had, in the hour which I usually set apart in the evening for retirement, a temptation to leave it, or halve it; but I solemnly went to my dearest Lord, and had access to His throne. I prayed much for my people, to whom I was going to speak, and told the Lord I could not go out of my room to the pulpit, except He would go with me. He gave me a gracious promise, and in His name I went forth; and, O, what a time I had! Never did I realize so much of God's presence before; my soul, as it were, left the body; I forgot earth, for I had my Jesus every moment with me. The people felt the word very powerfully. Lord, I believe we shall never forget this season. O, how did my Father hear my prayers! After supper and family duty, I retired to my closet, for the benefit of reading and prayer. I found my heart so engaged on the word of my Father, that I could scarcely prevail on myself to put it down. I put it down and took it up again. O, what sweet and interesting views I had of Christ and judgment to come! Blessed be God! I could meet Him this moment. All is peace within.

"Friday, 24th.—As usual, I awoke in some unknown hour of the night, and was found immediately on my knees. O, how sweet is prayer! I afterwards laid me down and slept again. In the morning, after family duty, &c., I rode to Gillingham, about three miles; the journey and the fatigue quite overcame me. I had many trials this day; but I brought them all to the Lord, and found His strength to be according to my weakness. I am confirmed in this experience once more, that I love

God with all my heart : did I not, I never could give up what I now do, without repining. O, the vast riches of the grace of God ! I spent the afternoon in my closet, in a profitable manner ; God, indeed, was with me. At tea-time, I had ———" (Miss Martha Raddon, afterwards Mrs. Crabb,) "to spend an hour or two with me. I believe we were all enabled to pass the time agreeably to God's will. I spent much time in my closet before preaching, and it was mostly spent in prayer for myself and congregation. I had much liberty and life from above, in declaring the glad truths of salvation. I spent nearly an hour after preaching, with my dear friend ; and we each prayed, perhaps twenty minutes, at parting.

"Sabbath day, 26th.—I was this morning, at an unknown hour, awoke, as it seemed to me, by some kind ministering spirit, and called to prayer ; for I remember last night, in my latest wakeful moments, I had a sweet sense of God, and especially of His angels, who I believe had a commission to guard my soul and body through the night. I found the exercise of prayer to be truly sweet. O, the richness of the grace of God ! I could not rise till near ten, being exceedingly ill and weak. Lord, sanctify this to my soul, and help me to rejoice in thee for ever ! About half-past ten I retired to my closet, and found an immediate spirit of prayer in the words, 'I beseech thee show me thy glory.' At twelve, I again felt the spirit of prayer. How sweet is it to breathe out my soul to God ! I have at this time a very heavy trial upon my mind ; but am enabled to lay all upon the Lord. About two, I *staggered away* to the Lord's house, very weak indeed. I had a pleasing subject to open, and found much of the presence of my Master in the sacred employment. The people felt and wept, and some were comforted. This is the first time of our having a service in the afternoon ; we had many people. Lord bless Wilton, my dear native town ! O Lord, do the people good ! In the evening I preached, but did not feel so much power as in the afternoon ; but I believe God made the people to feel. After preaching I spent near two hours in my closet. O God, let not thy word fall to the ground ! I was very ill indeed when I went to rest ; but the Lord be praised that I am as I am !

"Saturday, 27th January, 1798.—I did not rise very early this

E

morning, as I was so ill. My spirits were very low owing to
my weakness; but I have enjoyed much of the Divine presence, and the sweetness of prayer. How did I pray that God
would take away and blast all my pursuits, plans, and intentions if they would in the least hinder my soul's progress. I
spent some happy moments with my dear family in the evening, and then retired to rest. I could not but observe how kind
my newly converted family were this day to a dear minister of
Christ who was taken ill at our house. There was nothing
good enough for him, and every one sought to wait upon him.
Oh, my God, thine is all the praise, and thou shalt have it all."

In reference to the last extract from his Diary, it may
be added, that there is every reason to believe that Mr.
Crabb's father and mother, brother and sister, were,
through his prayers and by his instrumentality, added to
the number of those who, through grace, shall be saved.

In the extracts already given from Mr. Crabb's Diary, reference is made to an attachment he had formed for Miss Martha Raddon, and in the month of January, 1798, he began
to think seriously of marriage. Her piety and Christian
deportment were of no ordinary character, and she was not
destitute of personal attractions. She was unquestionably
a suitable helpmate for a minister; but whether in Mr.
Crabb's then circumstances, being wholly dependent on
his father for support, a union with her was prudent might
reasonably have been questioned, and it is a matter of
surprise that his father should have sanctioned it. Many
were the trials to which it led, but they were far more than
counterbalanced by the blessings he obtained from his
union with her. Mr. Crabb dared not, however, take
any step, much less one so serious as that which he now
contemplated, without seeking Divine direction: and therefore, prior to any declaration of his intentions, he for many
weeks committed the matter in fervent prayer to the Lord,

and did not open his mind to Miss Raddon until he had reason to believe that he was not acting in opposition to the will of God. In the letter which he wrote to her declaring his attachment, and which bears date January, 1798, he told her that the qualities he sought for in a wife, were :—" First, that she was born of God's Spirit. Second, that she was in some measure gifted to speak for, as well as to think of, Jesus. Third, that she had a determination to visit the sick with him. Fourth, that she was willing to give away as much money to the poor and the cause of God as she could get ; he having made a covenant with God to give the tenth of all he possessed for ever, and as much more as he could spare. Fifth, that she was plain in her dress. And sixth, that she was moderate in household furniture and housekeeping, that neither the poor nor the cause of God should be robbed of their due." He further requested that before she gave him an answer she would take the matter into serious consideration, and for that purpose, set apart the next Sabbath for fasting and prayer. He proposed to meet her at the throne of grace at seven until eight in the morning, at one until two in the afternoon, at five until six in the evening, and at nine until ten at night ; and this was, doubtless, strictly complied with by both of them.

This letter appears to have met with a favourable response ; and from that time until they were united in marriage, they continually met for prayer and holy converse, and when absent they met in spirit at stated hours at a throne of grace, and read at appointed times the same portions of Scripture. They often visited together the sick and the afflicted, and she occupied her spare time in instructing the young and the ignorant.

Mr. Crabb's letters during this period were deeply

spiritual, and calculated (as they were designed) to the
edification of her who was to become his helpmate in the
Gospel; and had she not drunk into the same spirit with
him, she could have found no delight either in them, or in
his society.

He has recorded the manner in which he spent the day
previous to his marriage, and it is worthy of being
noted:

" April 4th, 1798.—This," he writes, " is the last day I am to
be a bachelor. In the evening I retired to my closet, where
I continued in uninterrupted devotion till about one o'clock in
the morning. I did not pray to know the will of my heavenly
Father, for in fasting and prayer, which have not been little
on either side, each of us has had a perfect manifestation of
the will of God. Indeed, each of us sees the step we are about
to take to be so important, that were it not clear to be the will
of God we could not engage in it. I had a very happy time in
communing with the Lord, till poor mortality failed."

His nuptials were solemnised at the parish church of Gillingham, and the day was not spent as bridal days usually
are, even by those who profess godliness, in worldly mirth
and foolish talking and jesting, but in a manner suited to
so solemn an occasion. Having married in the Lord, they
spent the day unto the Lord, and in looking up to Him
for that grace which they needed. In his Diary he thus
speaks on the morning of his marriage:

" 5th April, 1798.—My views in marrying are purely
spiritual. I seek a bosom friend and a helpmate in the cause
of God. I spent much happy time this morning before light
in the same room, where my beloved and I have prayed and
wept many times. Lord, make this a good day—a day of
prayer and praise! We shall have many of our dear friends
come up to the wedding, and sure I am Jesus will be there.
But, oh, how unworthy am I of so glorious a guest!"

" After the marriage," he writes, " we spent the morning in

prayer and singing, and had a solemn time. I felt a deep sense of God's presence—nothing rapturous, but solemn."

It having been arranged that Mr. and Mrs. Crabb should, after their marriage, reside with his father at Wilton, they proceeded to his house, and in recording his journey homewards he writes :—

"I know not that I ever enjoyed more of God than I did on my road to Wilton. Our conversation was heavenly and serious."

Of all the engagements entered into in this life, marriage, whether regarded in its results to the individuals themselves or to others yet unborn, is pre-eminently the most sacred and momentous. It augments the miseries or the joys of this life; it adds to the bane or the welfare of society—it may be of the world at large—and to the number of those who shall hereafter awake up to everlasting glory or everlasting shame. But, alas! how often is it contracted, even by those who profess the Christian character, under the influence of improper motives, without due reflection and without Divine direction. That the men of this world should thus act is not surprising ; but that those who claim the Christian character should become " unequally yoked"—prefer gold to grace—personal attractions to Christian loveliness—is so dishonouring to God, that it seldom fails to bring with it the punishment it deserves. Happy that man who, like Mr. Crabb, seeks a helpmate from the hands of God, and receiving one from Him, lives with her in Him, to His glory.

CHAPTER VII.

Chapel built at Wilton.—Preaches there.—Renounces ministerial character —Becomes a partner with his father.—Fails in business—Trials —Opens a school.—Diary.—Discipline.

THE congregation which assembled in the room at Wilton, and to which reference has been made in the preceding extracts, having now become too large for the place, Mr. Crabb determined to build a chapel for their accommodation; and a piece of land having been obtained, a chapel was erected capable of holding 500 persons, which was opened for public worship on the 15th July, 1798, in connexion with the Wesleyan Methodists. In the erection of this building Mr. Crabb had to contend with great difficulties, and notwithstanding the most strenuous efforts were made to obtain the necessary funds, there remained on the day it was opened a debt to be provided for. It was his intention to make over the chapel to the Wesleyan Conference, upon the usual trusts; but as they were unwilling either to discharge the debt or take it upon themselves, Mr. Crabb, by the advice of his friends and with the consent of those who subscribed to its erection (except a few only whose subscriptions he returned), vested it in trustees independently of the Conference. The chapel, however, though not belonging to the Conference, was in connection with the Wesleyan body, and its services were conducted by the itinerating preachers.

No sooner was the chapel opened for public worship, than the Independent minister of the town was stirred up to hostility against Methodism, and forgetting his Master's declaration, that "he who is not against us is on our part," preached two sermons against Methodism from the words, "Take heed *what* ye hear, and take heed *how* ye hear." This, however, served only to promote a spirit of inquiry, and brought many to hear Mr. Crabb who, probably, would not otherwise have troubled themselves about him. This opposition, however, greatly added to his trials, for he was a "son of peace," and knew that strife and contention were no less opposed to the spirit of Christ than a hindrance to the Gospel.

Mr. Crabb's health had now become so far re-established that he was able to preach in the newly-erected chapel once or twice on the Sabbath, and once or oftener during the week. He had, however, no settled plans, but he was unwearied in his endeavours to promote the spiritual welfare of the people at Wilton, and continued to labour amongst them until the birth of his first child, when, as he reaped no ministerial emolument, and kept himself from being burdensome to them, he began to feel that it was his duty to provide for himself and those who were now dependent upon him; and this was the more necessary, as his residence in his father's house was found to be no longer convenient. The Wesleyan Conference were not likely to employ him as a stated minister, and there was no other body of Christians with whom he was in any way connected. To have stood alone amongst a poor and needy people, who would rather have looked to him for help than have contributed to his support, would have involved him in difficulties, and brought discredit upon the Gospel; and therefore it became necessary for him to turn his thoughts to some occupation by which he might maintain himself and his family, even although he might be compelled to abandon his ministerial character. This was a great and sore trial; but it seemed, under existing circumstances, to be inevitable. He was in the hands of Him who knew the path he took, and who fits His people by a wise discipline for the future work he has in store for them. Men might have judged of him by his labours and zeal—by his self-denial and self-sacrifice—they might have listened to his prayers and his preaching, and pronounced him to be fully qualified for the work of the ministry; but the Lord saw what man could not see, and in all wisdom He was not only about to refine him in the " fire which is in Zion, and the furnace which is in Jerusalem," but to show him " great and mighty things which he knew not."

It was in these circumstances that Mr. Crabb received an offer from his father and elder brother to admit him as a partner in their business of clothiers, and being pressed to come to a decision, he determined, rather than be wholly dependent on his father for support, to accept their offer, and accordingly he became a partner in the firm.

Mr. Crabb had too much energy of character to embark in this new occupation, upon the success of which his subsistence depended, without throwing into it all the energies of his ardent mind; and this he did; but whilst he diligently exerted himself to promote its success, he was not oblivious of those labours in which he had spent so many years of his life, and which were still dear to him. He therefore continued to preach in the chapel at Wilton on the Sabbath days, and he and Mrs. Crabb devoted their spare hours to visiting amongst the poor, the sick, and the needy. By degrees, however, the claims of business engaged more and more of his time, and being frequently obliged to visit London, the hours he heretofore spent in spiritual exercises were otherwise occupied. The blessedness recorded in the Diaries of former years was no longer realized. " The spirt of the world," he records, " crept in upon me, and smothered my private devotions. My wordly prospects were of a deceptive nature. I grew vain in my imaginations, and proposed to myself things too high in worldly matters." Alas! how strikingly does this record reveal to us the snares which lie concealed in the paths of duty, and demonstrate the necessity of a watchful spirit in the ordinary pursuits of life. How solemnly does it warn us of the dangers of the world, and affectingly exhibit the " vanity of the creature." That one who had been so devoted to the Lord's service, and would seem, through faith, not only to have enjoyed the substance of things hoped for, but, as on eagles' wings upborne, to have looked into the very portals of the eternal world, should have to make so humbling a confession, is too painful to contemplate; but grace is a tender plant, unsuited to terrestial influences, and unless it enjoy the continual sunshine of heaven, and be refreshed by those waters that flow from beneath the throne of God, though its root can never decay, it sickens, droops, and fades. Mr. Crabb had not, however, given himself up to a life of ease and self-indulgence, neither did he tamper with sin nor seek the friendship of the world. He was still a man of prayer—still held fast faith and a good conscience—and it may be doubted whether the worldliness and deadness of which he complains were not far preferable to the religion of many, who in this day claim communion with the saints, figure in devotional assemblies, and take the lead in religious meetings.

In the year 1802, the treaty of Amiens having opened

the ports of France to this country, Mr. Crabb, with a
view to establish a foreign trade, took a journey to Holland,
and from thence travelled through Flanders and France;
but his expectations proved abortive.   The foreign trade
he hoped to establish was never realised; losses, the result
of the late war, and the change of fashion, which deterio-
rated their stock, came on his father's firm; their credit
became damaged—business fell off—accommodation bills
were put into circulation, and, as might be expected, and
as happened to many who were ruined in like manner,
bankruptcy followed; although, as I am credibly informed,
there were assets, could they have been realised, much
more than sufficient to have satisfied every creditor.   In a
record left by Mr. Crabb, he says:

> " I cannot help referring to my final examination.   I was so
> conscious of my integrity, and so filled with assurance that God
> would bring me through all my trials, that I appeared more
> like a person going to a wedding than to a final examination
> under a bankruptcy.   How often have I, in looking back,
> thought with sorrow on that passage, ' My son, despise not
> thou the chastening of the Lord.'   O, my God, forgive my past
> sins !   It had been more to the credit of religion, had I been
> suitably affected with my position ; and I believe had I been
> so, my subsequent troubles would not have been so heavy and
> so lasting."

Having obtained his certificate, James Crabb and his
wife, with their children, who at this time were six in
number, retired to Salisbury, where for some time he
carried on the business of a dyer and seller of broad cloths;
but it was a hard struggle, and after enduring many trials,
he was obliged to relinquish it.   He then settled at Rumsey, and became a traveller for a firm in Gloucestershire,
in the broad cloth trade, by whom he was permitted to
sell on commission any commodity which did not interfere

with their business. In this new calling he had to endure much hardship and many trials; he was seldom in bed after five in the morning, summer and winter, and travelled daily from thirty to forty miles. He has left no record of the state of his soul at this period; but it appears that he continued to preach whenever he could, both in the week and on the Sabbath days, and allowed no opportunity of bearing witness for the truth, either by word or in the distribution of tracts, to pass unimproved. He was now under the discipline of Him who alone can "teach to profit"—principles were tried—sincerity was tested—patience was called into exercise—corruptions were detected, and the recesses of his heart made manifest. And so strongly did he feel this, that he has recorded, that he feared the loss of his trials, because he had learned so much from them.

After continuing this course of life for a period of two years, he relinquished it, and opened a school at Rumsey, for the instruction of boys in the ordinary routine of an English education. In the course of a short time he obtained a large number of pupils; and several of them being boarders, he took a larger house near the town, and engaged an able assistant. A new era in his life was now begun. The education of youth was, in his view, no light matter; he was anxiously solicitous for the spiritual welfare of his pupils, and knowing that the true way to fit men for the duties of this life is to educate them for heaven, he set before them the Gospel, in the hope of winning them to Christ. And he did not pray or labour in vain; several of them having, in after life, given testimony that through his instrumentality they had laid hold on eternal life.

He continued thus employed in the education of youth

many years; but, during the whole of this period, he preached on the Sabbath days at Rumsey, or elsewhere, and spent his spare hours and vacations in endeavours to promote the spiritual condition of its inhabitants and the vicinity.

The following extracts from his Diary exhibit the state of his mind during several of the years of this period of his life:

"2nd February, 1818—I am like a cypher. When shall I be as a light to lighten others—as a city set upon a hill? How glad should I be to preach the everlasting Gospel every day! Lord, direct my steps to Thee, and never let me move without Thee! Bless my dear children, and those placed under my care! I fear, sometimes, I am toiling and praying for nothing; but it cannot be, for the bread cast on the waters shall not be lost. These children will one day love Thee."

Again, he writes:

"Christ is mine with his glory eternally! I cannot fear— I cannot doubt, whilst I have such discoveries of Jesus Oh, that I may be more useful! I do not wish to go solitarily to heaven. Oh, that more would go with me! Lord, give me my dear children and dear pupils."

On the 18th August, 1820, he writes:

"Our lives are cast in pleasant places; we have a goodly heritage, but what an ungrateful heart do I possess! I have had strong impressions to give up preaching and my school, because I see so little fruit from my labours I fear, however, there is a mixture of pride and impatience in this. Lord, thou knowest O, make me holy!" He adds, "I have not been on the Mount for a long season, having had such awful views of my unfaithfulness, short comings, and the little resemblance I bear to Jesus—but, blessed be God, Christ was never more precious to me than now I desire to live in and on Him every moment. My soul clings to Him, and I live on His atoning blood and by His intercession. I feel in general a deadness to the world, and sweet composure of mind in the contemplation of the glory to come.

"31st January, 1821.—I have felt a growth in grace for two months past. My will is more lost in God. I sink into nothing before Him. O, adorable Redeemer, how precious art Thou to me! . . . . My heart is more drawn out in love to God and man, and is more simple in its aim. How solid and settled is my peace! All is tranquillity within, for I triumph over myself. I live—yet not I, but Christ liveth in me. Because He lives, I shall live also.

"9th October, 1821.—Sweet peace and love fill my heart—O, what a Father in Christ is mine! This day I have ordered nearly 200 tracts; intending to sew five or six together, and lend them, and afterwards to see the people weekly, and converse with them, and exchange tracts. This is better than giving tracts. Lord, help me! O, how I need to pray, and depend on God for Divine assistance!

"24th November.—I love to see the time I have been so long waiting for, when hundreds of tracts are distributed amongst my hearers. I get one farthing per week for the use of five tracts, to be changed weekly; and I have nearly 100 readers, besides the poor, to whom I lend gratuitously. By these means I am able to introduce fresh tracts, magazines, Baxter's 'Call,' Alleine's 'Alarm,' &c. O, my God, bless these means by giving us conversions! Blessed be God, our congregations in Rumsey increase. O, when shall I see the people converted to God?"

From the following extracts from his Diary, we may see how greatly his afflictions had, through a supply of the Spirit of Jesus, been sanctified and made profitable to him, in the subduement of self, in the rectification of his judgment, in deeper discoveries of his own corruptions, and in preparing and fitting him for the work which he was yet, through grace, to accomplish:

"25th February, 1822.—God has been deepening his work in my soul for months past. I know it from the sense I have of my weakness and nothingness. I am less than nothing: God has sanctified my affections and subdued my will. . . . . I feel for souls as I never felt before. The time is coming when

I shall (I think) be wholly given to God in my labours. O Lord, give me unerring direction !

" Monday, 12th March, 1822.—Oh ! God, forgive my unfaithfulness. I long to be as Thou wouldst make me. I feel myself unfit for the ministry, and am tempted to give it up ; but I hope to die in the work My soul presses after holiness, and pants with intense desire to be useful. . .   . I have had a refreshing, but humbling time, in finishing the 'Life of Brainard' Surely, I am less than the least of all saints.

"My heart sometimes strives to shift off duty , but God helps me Oh, how I need the Spirit's teaching and the Spirit's help ! Oh, the goodness of God, in pardoning my sins ! I reflect, with horror, on my past ingratitude and unfaithfulness. Oh, for more love and zeal to my gracious God ! I *must*, I *will* be wholly the Lord's Oh, take all that I have ! Swallow me up in Thyself ! Sanctify me wholly !

" 22nd July, 1822.—The latter part of my (school) vacation was spent in travelling, and preaching the good word of the kingdom. Rode to Swannage, forty-two miles, to preach a sermon, with a view to improve the death of a *very poor* woman, who lived and died in the Lord. I was well repaid for my journey, by the blessings I received in the service of my God."

CHAPTER. VIII.

AMONGST the places around and in the neighbourhood of Rumsey, where, during his leisure time, and on the Sabbaths, Mr. Crabb preached, Southampton, which was seven miles distant, and where in former years he had laboured during his itinerancy, was not lost sight of. This was the most populous town he visited, and it was, probably, spiritually, the darkest. Like most sea-port towns in those days, it was a den of iniquity. Being much grieved in his spirit at what he saw amongst the lower classes, he spent much time in visitation and the distribution of tracts amongst them ; and whenever opportunity offered he preached in the town.

In the year 1822, a clergyman of the Church of England being struck with the spiritual exigencies of the town, engaged the large assembly-rooms for a Sabbath service, which was numerously attended by the common people. These services having being discontinued, Mr. Crabb, seeing that the multitudes were as sheep without a shepherd, was deeply impressed with the idea that the Lord had "Called him to preach the Gospel unto them:"

but he was no longer the ardent and enthusiastic youth of 1795. His matured judgment led him to deliberate before he took so important a step as that which he now contemplated, and to wait until he should hear a voice saying unto him, " This is the way, walk ye in it." After much deliberation and prayer, he came to the determination of giving himself wholly to the ministry of the word, believing that he was called to do so:

"I see," he records, "more clearly than ever, that I am called to labour entirely for God, in the office of a pastor. I cannot describe the long and painful struggle I have had respecting this. I have just entered on my forty-ninth year, but should my life be spared a few years, and I am faithful, I may do much for God."

His journeys to Southampton were now very frequent, and, finding the field of labour before him greater than he could attend to whilst he continued his school, he determined to relinquish it to his two sons, (who then assisted him in carrying it on, and whom he had educated with a view to their becoming his successors,) and to offer himself to the Wesleyan Conference as one of their regular preachers. Such being his determination, he wrote to the Wesleyan superintendent of the Southampton district, stating his desire of hiring the old assembly-rooms for Sabbath services; another room for a weekly service in a densely populated part of Southampton, known by the name of Kingsland; and another room near the quay, for a weekly service amongst the sailors and custom-house officers of the port, the duties of the latter, rendering it obligatory on them to continue at their post during the Sabbath. In this letter he observed:

"A question arises, can I thus act in union with the Methodists? If so, it will afford me unspeakable pleasure, in the decline of my life, to give the remainder of my days to a people with whom I have been united more than thirty years, and who have had all my juvenile and best days ; but if not, I have counted the cost, and the sacrifice to me will be very great ;—namely, an end to an external union with a people I dearly love. I may be mistaken in my present views ; but of this I am certain, that my eye is single, and is fixed on one object—viz., the salvation of sinners ; and should it prove, by God's rejecting me, as an instrument of good to man, that I erred in my way, I hope to humble myself on account of my imperfections ; but shall never have to sorrow because I asked not counsel of God, or did not wait patiently for it. I have hitherto laboured with the rest of my local brethren, free of all earthly reward, and probably must for some time, even in Southampton, as the poor of the alleys, courts, and passages will, I hope, share the greater part of my labours. Of this I am certain, that I am influenced by no one, in any of these measures. I will neither make, nor head any party ; but expect to stand entirely alone, except we can remain united. No promises influence me, except those which I believe God has given me. I am anticipating no bodily ease, but an increase of labour ; no riches, no fine places of worship, or gay congregations ; but my prayer is, How shall I win souls to Christ? These measures are not adopted to me, because I am a disappointed man, or rejected of my brethren, for with my increasing years, the union existing between me, and the preachers, and the people, has mutually increased ; neither is the yoke of discipline in the Connexion grievous to me. If we cannot act together, my sacrifice will be truly great and painful. Rumsey, not a little loved by me, will lose my present labours ; but that loss can be supplied by a third preacher, who ought to reside in the town, and direct his pastoral labours to our society and congregation, and to the villages of the New Forest ; the latter of which are buried in moral darkness. To the support of which minister I will lend my influence, and join my mite according to my ability."

Shortly after this letter was written, Mr. Crabb attended a circuit-meeting of the preachers and class-leaders of the district, when he proposed to relinquish the school he then carried on and to engage as a third preacher on the Portsmouth circuit, at a yearly salary of seventy pounds, the whole of which he had every probability of obtaining without drawing from the funds of the Conference. The voice of the meeting was highly favourable to this proposal, and it was arranged that upon being appointed he was to divide his time between Southampton and Rumsey. He undertook to guarantee the rent (fifty-two pounds per annum) of a room, to be hired for preaching in Southampton—to make the regular collections for the benefit of the Society; and in order that the preachers' collections should not be injured, he stipulated to make no quarterly collection for the expenses of the room.   Such was his disinterested proposal; but happily for him and for Southampton, his proposal was slighted, and ultimately came to nothing. This terminated his connection with the Wesleyan body, who in losing him were deprived of one of the most faithful, zealous, and valuable adherents they ever possessed.   But there was an overruling Providence in this.   A good man's steps are ordered by the Lord.   His work had been appointed by Him by whom

" The foreknown station of a rush is as fixed as the station or a king

" And chaff from the hand of the winnower steered as the stars in their courses."

In his present extremity, Mr. Crabb looked up for guidance and direction, and soon found the fulfilment of the promise to those who thus look: "I will guide thee with mine eye."   Being impressed with the conviction that Southampton was the place where he was called to labour, he opened his mind to his brother ministers at Rumsey and the congregation amongst whom he chiefly laboured, who, though much concerned to lose him, would not hinder him from following what he deemed to be the purpose of God, but said, like those of old, when some would have deterred the Apostle from going to Jerusalem, "The will of the Lord be done."

Mr Crabb was now, in his forty-ninth year, about to enter upon new and important labours. The zeal of former years had been sobered down in the school of disappointment—his judgment had become matured by experience—he possessed more " of the spirit of power, of love, and of a sound mind"—and was more "nourished up in the words of faith and of good doctrine." Those two important elements in a Christian's life—prayer and affliction—had, through " a supply of the spirit of Jesus," fitted him for the ministerial work to which he was now called, and thus qualified, he went forth " strong in the grace which is in Christ Jesus," to proclaim the unsearchable riches of Christ.

Having determined on the course he ought to pursue, Mr. Crabb relinquished his school to his two sons, reserving the spiritual instruction of the pupils and the general oversight of the whole. Having engaged the old assembly rooms at Southampton for two services on each Sabbath day, he issued a hand-bill inviting persons of every Christian denomination to attend his first service, when he proposed to give them an account of what he aimed to accomplish. A large concourse of people was gathered together at this meeting, to whom he preached from the words—" The harvest truly is great, but the labourers are few." He appears to have preached with great power, and perceiving that his address had made some impression upon his audience, he begged that none who were present and connected with other congregations would come there again, but use their influence with those of their neighbours, who never went to the house of God, to attend his Sabbath day's services.

In the course of a few weeks his congregations became numerous and regular in their attendance, and he had every reason to believe that he was not labouring in vain. He was not, however, satisfied that he was doing all that he could do for Southampton, and therefore he preached several times in the course of the week out of doors and in licensed rooms hired by him in various parts of the town, by which means he became known to the people, and the number of his hearers at the assembly-rooms was much augmented.

Many were the difficulties he encountered in these attempts to carry the Gospel into the strong holds of Satan ; but he found *that* Gospel " mighty through God" to the " pulling them down." One of the licensed houses in which he preached was in a depraved quarter of the town, where the people offered him so much opposition, and endeavoured in so many ways to interrupt his services, that he was well nigh giving them up ; but he went on in faith, and by "long suffering, by kindness, by love unfeigned, by the word of truth, and by the power of God," overcame their enmity, and it was ultimately manifest that his " entrance in unto them was not in vain," many of them having been brought to the " knowledge and love of God."

Mr. Crabb received no emolument for these labours amongst the poor, nor did he expect any. He sought them, and not theirs ; but as the people who attended his ministry contributed nothing towards the expenses of worship, he took an early opportunity of telling them that although he asked nothing for himself, he expected they would contribute weekly, as God had prospered them, towards the necessities of the destitute and sick. To this appeal a response was soon made. The first weekly contribution amounted to five shillings, and these gatherings went on augmenting till they amounted, with additions made to them by Christian friends, to twenty shillings and sometimes thirty-five shillings per week,—a large sum, considering the class of people who contributed, and affording a proof, not only of the power of his preaching, but of the people's attachment to him.

The following extracts from the Diary which he kept at this time will show the extent of his labours, and the success which was vouchsafed to them :

" After preaching four weeks in this place, I find hundreds attending my ministry, and the number is increasing. God is getting at the hearts of the unhappy. Many who hear me are gathered out of the world, so that other churches and congregations are not robbed.

" 31st October, 1822.—I began this evening a weekly lecture, and had upwards of two hundred hearers. This is the second day of my pastoral visits. Visited about ten families, particularly the sick ; walked back to Rumsey at night, but did not reach home until past one in the morning. It was a trying day ; having first walked nearly all the way to Southampton, eight miles, to my friend's house. Oh, that I may be useful ; I wish to be wholly the Lord's.

" 4th February, 1823.—I feel greatly encouraged in God's work ; five hundred attend my ministry already. There is a good work on the hearts of many of my hearers, and some of the most profligate are reformed. Many and great have been the persecutions I have endured. My congregational collections, with donations of Church people, amount to upwards of twenty-six shillings weekly, which I distribute amongst the poor and sick of all denominations. I read a monthly report of the distribution of the money, and state the experience and conversation of each person I visit without mentioning names.

It excites great interest in the minds of the people. My exercises of late have been very great ; my character has been traduced, and my misfortunes of eighteen years since brought up to hinder my usefulness. Whilst ' Others are for war, I give myself unto prayer,' and nothing hurts me. I spend much of my time in visiting my hearers, and all the sick and distressed people I can hear of. My body is graciously supported as my journeys are frequent, and I am walking and visiting all day when in Southampton. I never felt my weakness more, and yet was never more devoted to God ; surely God is with me of a truth, and whilst my own dear people, with whom I have been united more than thirty years, look shy upon me, the clergy and Dissenting ministers give me their hands, and we live in love. On the last Sabbath I preached a sermon to the poor. The house was crowded, and God was with us.

" 16th February, 1823.—This Sabbath was a good day. God was with me. I am confident many are deeply awakened under the influence of God's spirit.

" I visited and relieved more than thirty families this week. The weekly subscription and donations amounted to three pounds and nine-pence. Seldom in bed until twelve o'clock, as I leave Southampton to return to Rumsey at ten o'clock, and often later. But the poor have the Gospel preached unto them, and they invite me in all parts of the town to visit them. If I would be a pastor, and be clear of the blood of my hearers, I must visit from house to house. On Saturday I visited a wretched family in great distress ; two were prostitutes. They did not attend any place of worship. I invited them to the house of God. ' No clothes,' was the excuse ; but they were at the house of prayer next day ; and the poor man has since had a new frock given him. We have brought many to God's house by thus visiting them."

It is evident from the preceding extracts from his Diary that Mr. Crabb's ministry had begun to tell upon the people, and that the plain, earnest, and affectionate manner in which he was accustomed to set the truth before them was not without success. It is written that when Philip went down to Samaria, and preached Christ unto them, there was "great joy in that city;" and thus it was at Southampton, where, through Mr. Crabb's ministry, the gospel was "glad tidings of great joy" to many.

Mr. Crabb had not ministered many weeks in the assembly-rooms before a circumstance occurred which greatly tended to the furtherance of the gospel. One Sabbath evening, after the termination of the services, he was requested to visit a young woman who was in dying circumstances. Upon reaching her wretched abode, which was in one of the worst localities of Southampton, he found her to be one of those unhappy beings "whose house is the way to hell," and who, having for three years lived an abandoned life, was now reaping the bitter fruits of sin. As he entered the room, she cried out, in agony of soul, "I want to go to Christ!" and imploringly asked whether He would receive her. This was a case for which Mr. Crabb was, from the tenderness of his heart, and his deep concern for perishing souls, peculiarly suited; and it pleased Him with whom there is plenteous redemption, to send home the word spoken by Mr. Crabb with power to her heart. Brought into the state of those of old who were "pricked in their hearts" by a sight of their sins, she was led by Him whose office it is to convince of sin, to that Saviour who has declared that He will in no wise cast out any that come to Him. At His feet she found pardon and peace; and, like the Corinthian thieves, adulterers, and covetous ones, whose cases are recorded for the encouragement of the vilest, was washed, sanctified, justified by the name of the Lord Jesus, and by the Spirit of our God. The glorious change thus wrought in this poor prodigal induced Mr. Crabb to have her removed to the house of a pious widow, where she received those consolations which could be afforded by those only who have learnt to weep with them that weep, and to rejoice with them that rejoice. During the few days she languished, she was visited by many of her former associates, whom she solemnly warned to flee from the wrath to come. One of them, through her testimony, was brought to seek forgiveness of her sins, and having obtained mercy, received an inheritance among them that are sanctified in Christ Jesus, and became, through Divine grace, an eminent witness for the Lord, and died a few years since, in the full assurance of faith.

After languishing a few weeks, this penitent sufferer died. Her funeral, at which Mr. Crabb officiated, was attended by hundreds of the people ; and had it not been an exceedingly wet day, it is supposed (such was the interest which her conversion excited) that thousands would have been present.

On the Sunday evening after her death, Mr. Crabb, being desirous of improving the event, preached a funeral sermon, in the large assembly-room, from the text, " Likewise I say unto you, there is joy in the presence of the angels of God over one sinner that repenteth." The room, which held nearly 1,000 persons, was thronged, and some hundreds, who were unable to obtain an entrance, went away. Proverbs v. and vii., and Psalms xxxix., li., and xc. were substituted for the lessons and Psalms of the day, and suitable hymns were chosen for the occasion. In consequence of so many having been excluded from the service, Mr. Crabb gave out after its termination that he would, on the next Sabbath evening, preach the same sermon, read the same lessons, and have the same hymns ; which he accordingly did, to a crowded congregation.

These services having created a great sensation amongst the lower classes, Mr. Crabb was desirous of still further improving the event which gave rise to them; and accordingly he published a narrative of the conversion of this young person, in the form of a tract, under the title of, " Jane Thring; or, the Penitent Magdalene." One thousand copies of this tract, though sold at 6*d*. each, were disposed of in Southampton in one week; and such was the interest it created, that it passed through seven editions.

The success which attended Mr. Crabb's efforts at this time, and the effects produced by the circulation of this tract, are thus recorded by him:

" 23rd February, 1823.—A blessed Sabbath. Read the service twice; preached three times; had an overflowing congregation in the evening. The people wept much; many are inquiring the way to heaven. I fear alarming without instructing them. O my God, give me wisdom, and that constantly! How good is the Lord! Felt no more fatigue at the end of the day than when I began. My congregations are increased about 150 since I preached poor Jane's funeral sermon, and the readers of the tracts, nearly twenty. O, that they may continue to feel and then act!

" 2nd March, 1823.—A good Sabbath; large congregations; much of God's power felt both by speaker and hearers; began explaining the Church liturgy, to be continued every Sabbath afternoon. In the evening, preached to parents. God was with me by His Holy Spirit. Could not leave our place of worship until nine o'clock in the evening. I have now upwards of 100 readers of tracts. God is doing much for Southampton. I feel my nothingness! I wonder that God has borne with me so long. I have been a cumberer of the ground. I fear my best performances have been attended with pride and vanity. O Lord, forgive!

" 10th March.—My trials have abounded. Spoke unadvisedly with my lips; that is, exhibited truth at an unhappy moment, and showed too much severity. O Lord, forgive me, and give me prudence in future!

" 26th March.—Visited five families in the country, truly

F

dark. One had a good heart , another had always loved God ; another was not so bad as others ; and another had such a family, she could not attend Divine service. My brother Joseph attended with me ; he brought all to kneel in prayer but one old pharisee , she resisted us in every way, telling us she was a Church woman, and would not change her religion Poor woman! I fear she had none to change! One of these poor aged sinners told us she had not been to church for twenty years past, yet she has gone into the town very often. How much the heathens at home need attention!"

CHAPTER IX.

THE conversion of Jane Thring, as narrated in Mr.
Crabb's tract, led many of her class to seek deliverance
from their degraded condition, and to Mr. Crabb they
naturally applied. Others might have excused themselves
by the pressure of other claims, the want of time and the
lack of means, but he was not a man to inquire " from
whence can a man satisfy these with bread here in the
wilderness?" but trusted in Him who fed the hungry
thousands with a few loaves and fishes, and with whom
" all things are possible." Having been made the honoured
instrument of bringing these perishing outcasts to a sense
of shame and a care for their souls, he *dared* not turn
them away : " He had compassion on them," and "took
them in." In a few days *eleven* of them had thrown themselves on his hands; and as there was at that time no
Penitentiary in the town, he placed them, upon his own
responsibility, separately, with persons willing to receive
them. Having undertaken this charge, which he was
unable to bear by his own means, he began not only to
look up but to look around for assistance. There lived at

that time in Southampton a retired physician, Dr. Lindoe, a man of God, whose heart was warm with love towards his fellow-men, and full of zeal in the cause of Christ. He was no stranger to Mr. Crabb, they were heirs of the same inheritance, and fellow-workers unto the kingdom of God. To him, therefore, Mr. Crabb communicated the circumstances in which he was placed, and he readily supplied means for the present support of these returning prodigals. Mr. Crabb's next step was to consult the Rev. Robert Heath, the then curate of All Saints',—a man of eminent piety, and whose memory is still revered by many in Southampton; and under his advice a house was hired by Mr. Crabb and Dr. Lindoe, which was fitted up as a temporary asylum, where these women were placed with a view to their ultimate restoration to society. These facts having been made known, subscriptions to a considerable amount were obtained for the support of the asylum and its inmates; but as these means were precarious, and an asylum upon a larger scale and permanent foundation was needed, Mr. Crabb laboured incessantly to interest the clergy and other influential persons in the town to co-operate with him and Dr. Lindoe in accomplishing so desirable an object. In this matter, however, he was appointed to endure many and sore trials. The disappointments and indignities he met with in the prosecution of this labour of love, even from those who were professing disciples of Christ, are in a great measure detailed in the following entries made by him at that time in his diary :

"7th April, 1823.—The clergy have deserted me in the matter of the intended Asylum. They will not follow a Methodist, although I propose to them to frame the whole plan according to their views. One was offended at my calling on him—a second denied himself—and a third withdrew his name after he had signed a requisition, stating that he could not live in hot water with his brethren. I have ten unfortunate women to protect and provide for, and only two friends to consult in all my plans. I even fear I shall not get a requisition. My heart is pained and discouraged at times ; but God supports me, and gives me great consolations.

"13th April.—This day I enter on my fiftieth year. Oh, my soul, nearly half a century gone, and but little done for God or mankind. Oh, my Father, quicken and stir up my soul. I had a good Sabbath ; I am going through the Lord's Prayer in the afternoon, and in the evening preaching a course of lectures on the Christian Sabbath. How much I need God's blessing on my labours—I can do nothing without it !

"24th April.—All difficulty in the Magdalene business. I have now nine to support, and must trust entirely to the future bounty of unknown friends ; for all, or at least all who should help, desert me—even the clergy and corporation. But God will bring me through every difficulty.

"5th May.—My difficulties make me low. No one to help me. Money wanted for the poor Magdalens—none coming—no public meeting—everyone despairs of success ; but God will help me. 'Tis needful I should be thus tried, to stir me up to prayer. My soul was deeply engaged after the labours of the day till near midnight in fervent and strong cries and tears.

"16th May.—Much dejected, but God can help. Obtained two names only to the requisition for the Mayor on behalf of a Penitentiary, though engaged all day. Men consult their worldly interests rather than the glory of God. Still discouraged. Sad untruths propagated respecting the poor Magdalens, and I do not escape. Dearest Redeemer, I can bear it all for Thee !

"Sunday, 18th May.—Returned home (from Southampton) at half-past eleven ; *retired to rest at one.*

"Monday, 19th.—*Rose about four.* Rode to Thruxton, eighteen miles, to preach to a friendly society. God gave me his Spirit almost without measure in prayer and preaching, both in the morning and evening. I had great wrestlings for poor Thruxton.

" Wednesday, 21st May.— All day in Southampton, canvass-
ing amongst the rich for a requisition to the Mayor for a public meeting on behalf of the Penitentiary. No success ; all
asleep, or dead. One, a member of Parliament, though horri-
fied at the account I gave him, thinks it needless to attempt a
cure. Another, a magistrate, pleads the necessity of prostitutes that our wives and daughters may not be insulted in the
streets. The clergy want to build a new church, and they
think it ill-timed to attempt to obtain money for the Asylum.
Others say it is wrong to get work for these people whilst the
industrious need it—so *that they must perish.* The High Church
party will not unite with me because I am a Methodist.
Others love their money more than precious souls. I am sometimes tempted to give up the work as impracticable ; but I
feel indescribable horror at the thought of this. How shall I
meet God at the last day. The expense of eleven females is
great. Few help me—many laugh at my burdens. Sometimes I am tempted to go home and live in comfort, fearing I
have missed my way. Oh, the heart-aches I have ! My rest
is in God. If he be for me, all is well. Yes, I am determined
to leave all for Jesus."

How touching are these aspirations of his renewed
heart ! They are emanations from the Spirit of Him
who is love, and are redolent with heavenly fragrance.
They bring before us the Christian as he is when alone
with God, and reveal not only the trials, but the triumphs
and exultations of faith. How blessed thus to live above
the tribulations of this life, and the things of time—to
see the hand of a reconciled Father in every trial and
disappointment, and to realise that nothing can separate
us from His love in Christ Jesus ! Oh religion, thou
choicest gift of heaven to fallen man ! What though
thou hast no form or comeliness to those who have no
vision to behold thy radiance, and no ear to listen to the
melody of thy voice, yet, to the believing heart, thou art
full of grace and altogether lovely ! Whatever there is of

blessedness in this sin-defiled world—whatever of glory, it comes from Thee! 'T is Thine to remove the burden of the heavy laden, to speak peace to the troubled, to bind up the broken in heart. Thy presence turns disappointment into hope, and tribulation into joy.—Thou smilest and the desert rejoices, and the wilderness blossoms as the rose. Thou lightest the martyr's dungeon with Thy radiant lamp, givest him songs in the night, and makest his fiery bed a flaming chariot to conduct him to his crown. Arrayed by Thee in garments of light, death comes a shining messenger to reveal to the departing saint visions of coming glory, and guide him through the grave into regions of endless day. O daughter of the skies—thou messenger of peace—thy triumphs shall not terminate with time ; for in that day when the tabernacle of God shall be with man, thou shalt attune the harps of ten thousand times ten thousand, and thousands of thousands to hymn the triumphs of Him who is the First and the Last. Thy power shall then be seen and known by those that despised thee, and thy worth shall be acknowledged to the praise of Him who gave thee thy brightness out of His fulness, and decked thee with His glory.

It was not long before the Southampton Asylum found many supporters ; and its resources having become enlarged, the number of its inmates became increased. All this was in a great measure the result of Mr. Crabb's exertions : but greater trials of his faith and patience yet awaited him. Amongst the supporters of the Asylum was Lord Edward O'Brien—whose benevolence was of a high order, and who not only subscribed largely himself, but interested others in its behalf. His Lordship was, however, one of those who, like many estimable Churchmen, entertained a strong prejudice against Dissenters; having learnt that Mr. Crabb, who took the lead in the management of the Asylum, and was the spiritual instructor of its inmates, was a dissenting minister, he began to fear that these perishing women might be made Dissenters, and objected to Mr. Crabb, or any other Nonconformist, having any further connection with the charity. Upon this being privately made known to Mr. Crabb (who loved peace, and was ready to make any sacrifice to secure it), he immediately withdrew from the Institution, which in a short time was supported by many of the aristocracy and persons of distinction, and was, *for a time,* one of the most flourishing institutions in the town. But the Asylum needed a sustaining power, which neither money nor great names could supply; and Lord O'Brien having died, the Institution soon after began to decay, and gave symptoms of dissolution. In this emergency the committee, who knew the value of Mr. Crabb's assistance, besought him to re-unite with them; which he, possessing much of that charity which "beareth all things, endureth all things, and is not easily provoked," immediately complied; and he continued his connection with the Institution until his death. Soon after his return to the Committee the erection of a Penitentiary having been deemed advisable, Mr. Crabb *volunteered* to obtain the necessary funds, and forthwith proceeded to the task. He not only waited upon the majority of the respectable residents in the counties of Hants and Wilts likely to contribute, but came up to London several times to obtain subscriptions from those whom he had long known to be ready to every good work. His long journeys on foot in all weathers, his privations, and the mortifications and insults he met with in the prosecution of this charitable work would have overcome many a stout heart; but though often cast down and sore broken, he was never subdued. He fixed his eyes upon his Master; remembering His disappointments, and knowing that His presence went along with him, he feared no man's face, and none made him afraid. In the course of a short time the Penitentiary was erected at the cost of £2,200, which was raised by subscriptions, the greater part of which were obtained by the laborious and persevering efforts of Mr. Crabb; and it is not too much to say that but for him it would never have been built. From the time it was opened, which was in the year 1823, it has been well supported, and up to the present time (1853) 425 unhappy beings have been admitted within its walls, most of whom have been reclaimed from a life of sin, and all of whom have "had the Gospel preached unto them." The management of the Institution is vested in a committee chosen from the subscribers : and the internal arrangements are under the direction of a matron and two superintendents. Prayers are read every morning and evening. On Wednesdays an address is given to the women, and on the Sabbath day there are two services. This Institution is a monument of Mr. Crabb's Christian philanthropy, and of his untiring labours on behalf of his fellow men,—an Institution of which Southampton might well be proud.

But the movement thus made on behalf of this unhappy class of our fellow beings was not confined to Southampton. Mr. Crabb's tract on the conversion of Jane Thring having been widely circulated, led to similar movements on their behalf in other populous places. In a short time the Portsmouth Female Penitentiary, and soon afterwards the Salisbury Female Penitentiary were erected, and, under God, have been the means of rescuing

many from the miseries of sin and destitution, and
bringing some of them to the feet of Him who has said
to them, as He said to one of old, who like them was "a
sinner,"—Go in peace.

Mr. Crabb still continued his Sabbath services at the
assembly-rooms; but although they were well attended,
there were yet some thousands in Southampton who
were never seen in a place of worship.   One of the most
depraved places was that part of the town called Kingsland, already referred to, and there Mr. Crabb established
a Sabbath-school, in which 100 children, taken from the
streets, were brought under Christian instruction.   The
next place to which he directed his attention was Itching
Ferry,—a small village, about one mile distant from
Southampton, inhabited by sailors and fishermen.   These
people were wholly destitute of all spiritual instruction :
for although there was a church in the village, the minister
not only did not preach the Gospel, but had no influence
with the people.   To them therefore Mr. Crabb determined to carry the word of life; but no sooner did
they hear that he was coming to preach to them than a
violent opposition was stirred up against him, and a
number of drunken sailors, who had been engaged in
a launch, got ready to oppose him on his first appearance
amongst them.   Nothing terrified, he took his stand upon
a pile of timber lying on the shore; and laying hold of
the arm of an anchor which was near him, he began by
telling them that he was the friend of fishermen and
sailors, and came to tell them the way to heaven.   Subdued no less by his firm and resolute bearing than by
the affectionate manner in which he addressed them, they
suffered him to preach to them : and such was the effect
of his address, that many who came to mock and insult

him showed him kindness, or treated him with respect. He continued to preach to these people every Saturday on the sea-shore, until he had not only overcome their enmity and opposition, but had so ingratiated himself with them that they at last came out of their cottages and boats to hear him; and many of them walked over on the Sabbath to join in the services of the assembly-room. The success which attended his labours at this place, induced one of the Dissenting bodies to erect a chapel for these people; and from that time, feeling that his ministrations amongst them were no longer needed, he discontinued them.

The sailors belonging to the port of Southampton were particular objects of Mr. Crabb's solicitude—they had no religion, and no man cared for their souls. Soon after he commenced his labours at Southampton, he formed an acquaintance with Captain Bazin, the commander of a vessel called the *Speedy*,—a man full of zeal in the service of Christ, and very earnest for the spiritual welfare of those who do business in great waters; and they laboured together for their improvement. The *Speedy* was, in every sense of the word, a Bethel; and whenever she was in the port of Southampton Mr. Crabb preached on her deck two or three times a week to the sailors who belonged to the ships then in the port; and as the vessel was moored close to the shore, many persons who were assembled on the quay were enabled to join in the service.

With Captain Bazin Mr. Crabb sailed once a year to Jersey; and during the voyage, whenever the weather permitted, he preached to the sailors, and they were summoned morning and evening to prayers. At Jersey he preached on the shore to the sailors, and went about the island preaching in the chapels, where he was always welcome.

The following extracts from his Diary will show how abundant he was at this time in labours for the benefit of his fellow-men, regardless of the revilings of the ungodly, and the cruel contempt of those from whom he might have expected encouragement:

"I expect a chapel in Kingsland will soon be begun. The clergy are much alarmed, and say, now ' We must build a new church, to save the people from being Dissenters.' *O that they were anxious to save them from the devil!* I preached in the evening at Kingsland, and reached home about half-past ten o'clock. O that I were more in earnest for the salvation of souls !

" Wednesday, 15th.—A day of great affliction: family trouble. No support in the Penitentiary. All men seem to discourage me ; the wicked persecute, and good people have but little faith. I am blamed for neglecting my sick and the poor, in attending to such wicked creatures. My faith and perseverance are called stubbornness ; but I dare not give up. I am dreadfully tempted of the devil. I have no prospect of a chapel in Kingsland-place. *The rich will do nothing ; in general, how much better to be poor !*"

The nature and extent of his labours at this time appears from a letter which he wrote to Dr. Winter :

" My labours," he writes, " I consider of a home missionary nature, as you will perceive when I describe them. On Sabbath days, I preach three times at the rooms. On Monday I preach at the Bethel. Tuesday at Hursley, to a large congregation of country-people and farmers, whose hearts appear to be prepared by the Lord. Wednesday at Kingsland, to a hardened, thoughtless people, of whom there are about 2,000, not one-fourth of whom attend any place of worship ; we have a good Sabbath-school there. Thursday at Southampton, through the summer in the environs of the town, in the waste places, or on board ship, or in the Bethel. On Friday at Rumsey. On Saturday I preach to that notoriously wicked clan, the Itching

Ferry fishermen and sailors, on their own shores. They not only now treat me with respect, but hear with great attention, and many, perhaps forty, come to the rooms on Sabbath days, though at a considerable distance from their dwellings."

Such were his astonishing labours—such his unwearied diligence in the service of Him who had sent him out "into the highways and hedges." He went forth daily to dig down into the lower strata of society; and often did he turn up that which was once uppermost, but which, by the convulsions and upheavings of society, had become lowermost. As the labourers who dig and search amongst the ruins of the once famed cities of Herculaneum and Pompeii bring to light the gorgeous column or splendid architrave, "the storied urn or animated bust,"—hidden treasure long buried in darkness,—so Mr. Crabb, as he dug daily amidst the ruins and rubbish of the fall, brought to light the hidden ones of God—broken hearts to be healed—souls which, though long buried in the depths of sin, were designed to be renewed by the Holy Ghost, and to become "as corner stones, polished after the similitude of a palace."

CHAPTER X.

Chapel needed for his hearers.—Out-of-door preaching.—Obtains
a site for his chapel.—Lays the first stone.—Diary.—His trials ,
—Obtains subscriptions.—Letters to Lady Orde.—Reflections.
—Pays for building his chapel

MR. CRABB'S ministrations at the assembly-rooms had
now continued for the space of thirteen months; and a
settled congregation having become formed, he began to
feel the necessity of a more convenient place of worship, and seriously to contemplate the erection of a
chapel for their accommodation. Another chapel was also
needed for the people at Kingsland, who assembled for
worship in a small room which would not hold one-half of
those who were willing to attend. He was encouraged to
attempt a supply of these wants by many of the friends
whom the Lord had given him for his encouragement, and
whose pecuniary contributions had from time to time greatly
assisted him in his various undertakings. He would not,
however, embark on so serious an undertaking without
deliberation. His feelings on the subject are recorded in
his Diary of this date, and serve to show the singleness of
his aim, and his earnest desire not to run before, but to
follow the leadings and direction of the Lord:

" Thursday, 20th May, 1823.—My mind is much depressed ;
I am tempted of the devil, and full of fears lest human feelings
should be mingled with my zeal for the Lord of Hosts. O my
God, save me from every wrong motive ! I am determined to

leave all for Jesus. I will be like the Apostles I know not
how I shall be provided for, but 'the earth is the Lord's and
the fulness thereof.' Much discouraged respecting my two
intended chapels those who have money will not assist. I
fear Kingsland place must be given up, and a Sabbath-school
of 100 children O God, help !—I can do no more. The poor
people have been applied to, and they have promised by pence
in the course of a year fifty pounds. The rich will do but
little ; but the poor are rich towards God they give their mite
willingly

"Thursday, 22nd May.—Canvassed all day for names (subscribers to his chapel) amongst the rich. Could do nothing
but with one gentleman of the Navy. My temptations were
horrid I shall never forget them ; but God helped. In the
evening preached at Kingsland place. I preached *to myself*
from 'God is in the midst of her, she shall not be moved God
shall help her, and that right early' How present God was
with me cannot be described by pen or tongue I felt wrapped
up in the glory of God, and faith was in lively exercise. O that
the people may cherish the feeling they then appeared to have
Reached home at twelve at midnight."

At this period Mr. Crabb continually preached out of
doors, for he felt that there was no other way of bringing
the Gospel to bear upon the great masses of those who
never entered a place of worship. There are, doubtless,
many objections to this method of preaching; but they
are far more than counterbalanced by its advantages. In
out-of-door preaching the people generally feel that the
preacher is in earnest—that he is concerned for their souls,
and is not performing a mere duty, or seeking his own
advantage. Its novelty creates an interest—it brings the
truth into the streets and lanes, into the inner circle and
to the fire-side—it makes it the topic of conversation and
the subject of thought. In short, it comes home to a man
in a way calculated to arrest his attention. In the present
day, when men insist upon the duty of following the

example of our Lord and his Apostles, it is not a little remarkable that this method of conveying the truth to the masses of the people has been so little practised and insisted on. It is objected that our Lord and his followers had no churches to preach in, and were obliged, from the necessity of the case, to preach in the streets and highways,—an objection which might be admissible if there were churches and chapels to preach in—but as it is notorious that if all the places of public worship throughout the land were filled on the Sabbath, there would be millions of men and women, who if they desired it could not obtain the means of grace—to that extent, at least, there is the same need now as in Apostolic days, to carry the Gospel to those who cannot or will not come to it. But men and women are suffered to live like heathens in a Christian land, and perish in their sins, because some ministers dare not, and others have not the courage or self-denial necessary to preach to them in the only way in which they can bring the truth before them. Mr. Crabb, however, had compassion on the rabble. Knowing the tremendous consequences of sin, he would not let them alone in their sins, but sought to win them by any means. Knowing that Satan's movements were aggressive, he went forward aggressively, attacked his citadel, and carried the war into his camp. Upon this subject he thus speaks in his Diary :

"I now preach out of doors every week. The polite part of the town wonder at my imprudence in preaching to such a miserable set of sinners, and I offend many thereby ; so did Jesus and the great revivers of the last century. I am persecuted through every street I walk on account of my having exposed the sins of the people ; but God supports me. I have not been so honoured for more than twenty-eight years. Oh that I may be worthy of this, and imitate Jesus more and more !"

It appears from his Diary that in the prosecution of this part of his labours he met not only with opposition from those whom he calls " the respectable part of the town," but from the people themselves to whom he preached ; and often nothing but his firm bearing and kindness of manner, under God, saved him from personal violence.   On the 10th September, 1823, he records :

> " Went to Southampton ; preached in the open air, on the spot whereon I stood the last week   The persecutors were there, with pipes, tobacco, and strong drink.   They sat quiet, and heard the whole of the service.   It was done unto me according to my faith.   As I was returning home to Rumsey, I was sent for to visit a man who has long despised the Gospel, now almost senseless   Eleven persons were there, and I endeavoured to catch the opportunity to do good.   O Lord, bless the poor sinners !   Arrived home about eleven o'clock."

Mr. Crabb having determined to build a chapel, and an eligible site having been found, he entered into a contract with a builder, who agreed to erect and complete it for £2,200; of which £600 was to be paid in two years, and the remainder as Mr. Crabb could get it.   The circumstance, and his feelings on the subject, are thus mentioned in his Diary :

> " This day, fixed with the builder relating to my new chapel.   God knows the responsibility I have taken on me, to beg £600 in two years.   Nature shrinks, and some will judge me imprudent ; but the Guide of my youth will be the support of my old age and prosper my undertaking.   I feel the burden at times , but I can cast it on my God, and it is all well.   In general my soul is very happy in my God, and my communion with Him uninterrupted."

On the 11th of September, 1823, the foundation-stone was laid—but he stood alone on that day.   No minister of the town, although they were all invited to attend, was present.   " He followeth not with us," was the cry then with many, as it is now, and was in the days of the Apostles, and the attempt to save souls meets with little sympathy from many, except it is found in connection with a party or a sect. Few are the men who would not have been discouraged by this circumstance; but Mr. Crabb had not put his trust in an arm of flesh. His aim was to be the honoured instrument of bringing souls to Christ, and he well knew that in the path of duty the Lord would neither leave nor forsake him. The circumstances attending the laying of the first stone of his chapel are thus narrated by him:

"This evening I attended Divine service on Castle Hill, when we laid the first stone of a building, to be named Zion Chapel. I was obliged to go through the whole ceremony of mason and to address the people, without any minister to support me. My dear brothers, Reynolds of Rumsey, and Adkins of Southampton, were from home; my brother Fowler was fearful of offending Conference, as they considered that I had set up in opposition to them; and my dear brother Draper, the Baptist minister, felt much of the same spirit. He was solicited to preach, but he complained of his voice; but his presence only there would not have hurt his voice. One of his deacons was on the Hill, loudly proclaiming that I had come there in opposition to the Methodists, and that it would all crumble to atoms; that I had emptied Rumsey Chapel already, and then deserted it. If he had said that I found it with a debt of nearly £1,900 on it, and by the plans which I proposed, and which, in unison with my brethren, I followed up, the debt was reduced to £750, it would have been nearer the truth. He also adverted to the fact, that no minister would preach for me. O Lord, help me to pray much for this false witness!

"My mind has been much exercised by these things, and I · have felt a disposition to fear lest I should not raise the £600 in two years, which I have promised to pay the builder. My temptations were violent. Gladly would I have given up all my toil for ease, but I dare not. My soul is struck with horror

when I contemplate it. Let my Saviour be with me always as
He now is:

> 'Then I can smile at Satan's rage,
> And face a frowning world!'

But it is not the world, or methinks I could bear it better ;
it is God's way. O Lord, strengthen me, and all will be well !
I have, with these trials, been followed with the most horrid
temptations to infidelity, and Satan has been like a lion against
me. When in the height of my distress I prayed for my persecutors, and pleaded with God for a promise of support, I had
the following given me with power : 'No weapon formed
against thee shall prosper, and every tongue that riseth up
against thee thou shalt condemn'

"After the ceremony of laying the stone, I ascended the
platform, which was unexpectedly prepared for me, and
preached to a large congregation, who were chiefly the poor ;
but, O ! they are my inheritance, for I am sent chiefly to them
I feel that I am perfect weakness ; I am like a reed, yea, a
bruised reed ; but God will help me, and 'bring forth judgment
unto victory' I had a most delightful season in preaching from
'Thy kingdom come.'

" 15th.—At six in the morning, and at six in the evening,
had to met the tradesmen who are concerned in building my
chapel. O what a system is trade brought to—what art,
cunning, and deception It is the love of money How can
they love God, who love the world ? It is impossible

" 18th —Preached at Three Field, by moonlight. My late
persecutors were amongst the congregation. Oh that they may
be brought to God. Returned home a little before twelve
o'clock, P M.

" 22nd.—Heard to-day that the poor sailors to whom I
preached on Saturday were much pleased, and intend hearing
me again ; and that many more attended the dissenting place
of worship on Sabbath day. My mind is much exercised
about the new chapel. How will it be paid for ? Every one
wonders at my imprudence in building without money, or any
church union with others. But my faith is generally lively
and active, and that brings me through many difficulties.

" God shall be with me in all my difficulties. I have but

£10 towards £100, which must be paid in a few days. I hear that my enemies rejoice in the prospect that I shall not prosper ; but who can hinder it, if God be with me ?

"The worst that my opponents say, amongst those who call themselves religious, is that I do all I am doing to gain a name. O Lord forgive them for assuming thy prerogative of reading and knowing my heart. Every opponent and enemy has my pity and my prayers ; none can harm me while my communion with God is so uninterrupted and delightful.

"24th.—Ill with a violent headache, but happy in God. I feel God, my Father, nearer and dearer to me than language can describe. I have had dreadful temptations of late relating to the truth of Scripture and the moral government of God. How sweet were those words to me when rising from my bed, after an hour's sweet communion with my God, 'I love the Lord because he hath heard the voice of my supplication, and he hath inclined his ear unto me, therefore will I call upon him as long as I live,' Psalm cxvi. 1, 2. My joy was not ecstatic, but my peace and assurance were deep, and inconceivably great."

But he was appointed unto the afflictions which he has thus recorded, and he received them as designed for a trial of his faith and patience. The world loves its own ; but Jesus, and those who love Him, it hates. It is no wonder, therefore, that Mr. Crabb was hated by the world, and that his character, as a man and a minister, was assailed with the bitterest rancour ; but as the Ark was lifted nearer to heaven as the floods fell upon it, so the more the Christian is assailed "by the floods of ungodly men," the nearer is he borne upwards towards Him who is "a hiding-place from the wind and a covert from the tempest."

Mr. Crabb's chapel being now in the course of erection, it was necessary for him to be prepared for the pecuniary engagement he had undertaken. He did not, however, expect to raise so large a sum as £2,200 without many painful and laborious efforts; and therefore whilst he exercised faith he looked to the means, and expected through them the assistance he needed. Having set to work in the right way, and cast all his care upon the Lord, who had shown him, by many proofs, that He cared for him, he entertained no misgivings as to the result. His applications, by letter and in person, to individuals of all ranks—from the then Sovereign of these realms to the humblest person who could lend a helping hand—were unparalleled. It is computed that he travelled some thousands of miles on foot, and wrote many hundreds of letters. The privations and fatigues he endured in accomplishing this work were incredible. I have been told that, when in London, he was one day so overcome by fatigue as to be compelled to retire into the Royal Exchange to rest upon one of the seats; where, having fallen into a deep sleep, he was discovered by a gentleman to whom he was known, and who, thinking he was ill, awoke him. Upon being asked why he did not engage a vehicle to carry him from place to place; he replied, that the money was given to him for another purpose, and that his chapel wanted all the money he could get. On another occasion, he was found by a friend in the back court of a leading thoroughfare, whither he had retired to eat his dinner of bread and cheese. From circumstances like these we see that he was influenced by higher considerations than those which spring from the things of time, and thus was enabled to triumph over self-interest, self-pleasing, and self-indulgence. The two following letters, written by him to his kind benefactress and friend, the Lady Elizabeth Orde, whose counsel and sympathy solaced him in many of his trials and disappointments, and whose pecuniary assistance helped forward his many Christian designs, will serve to show some of the privations he endured in his endeavours to raise the money he needed for his chapel, and how often he had cause to say, " Vain is the help of man :"

" Bath, 18th March, 1825.

" MY DEAR LADY ELIZABETH,—I received your last favour from Heythrop. Every note gladdens my heart, because you sorrow with me when I sorrow, and rejoice with me when I can tell you of God's great goodness to me. I ought to be more thankful for the help I get; but how glad shall I be when I have begged the remaining debt of almost £1,000, to free this chapel for my poor dear people ; for though it is a duty I must discharge, yet how many useful and profitable visits do I lose amongst the poor, &c. I find, moreover, that the business I am engaged in is worldly ; it is to get money to pay for a building : but then I have this consolation—it is for the glory of God ; and I am often introduced to many very pious people, who I believe will pray for me.

" I preach but little while I am from home. The Dissenters suspect me. The church cannot employ me ; and the Methodists feel wrongly towards me, because I have left their great body, to try to do a little good, which I could not do upon their plans. O, when shall we love as brethren ! A few poor people opened an underground kitchen for me in Bath, when I told them of the adorable Redeemer. On Saturday I walked the greater part of the way to Wells, and was much fatigued. On Sabbath day, I heard the son of a Scotch bishop twice at the Cathedral at Wells. Dear youth, he preached faithfully the fall and salvation by Christ. He is doing much good. I called on him on Tuesday, and he gave a guinea to the chapel. I have been very poorly since I have been in these parts ; my journeys, &c., have been too much for me. I was confined to my bed nearly all day on Monday ; but on Tuesday I had an engagement which was made a week before, and I attempted to perform it on horseback, as it was not a coach-road. The distance was nearly forty miles to and from the place ; *but I met with £2 for the chapel.*

" London, 19th April, 1825.

" Eight or nine days have gone since I heard from you. I

hope all is well, as it is when God is with us. I have been tried with disappointments since I have been here, but it is all for the best. The promise will never fail, nor will God disappoint me in the end, but He will help in his own way. I have obtained but £7 10s during the last eight days, five of which a captain F. Vernon gave me. I have walked a great deal since I have been in town, but have been kindly supported. Yesterday I walked full eight hours, and felt much disappointment. I got no dinner, and went to bed supperless, *fearing I should spend the poor's money* before I got it; and yet I think I went too far, because my heavenly Father will not forsake me."

There is something deeply affecting in these letters. Here is a man of God wandering from city to city and town to town, and going from house to house, in the attitude of a beggar, to ask support from the disciples of Jesus, in his endeavours to make known the tidings of His salvation to perishing sinners. Worn out with fatigue, cast down by disappointments, and grieved by cruel discouragements, day by day and week by week bearing indignities and insult, neglect and unkindness, even from those who ought to have given him encouragement and support, he painfully gathers together the sum he needs for his Divine Master. What a sight is this for angels,— for Christ himself, to look down upon! How humbling to the disciples of Him who gave to them His all! How many, who turned a deaf ear to his tale, and would not look into his case, had they known his heart and the motives by which he was influenced, would have thought it a privilege to hold up his hands, shorten his labours, and help onward his work; but they lost the blessing which would have been theirs in thus doing. Alas! how prone are the best of men to refuse their help in a good cause, —towards that which is for God's glory,—because they cannot secure success, forgetting that they have nothing to do with results. The endeavour is theirs, the success is with God. What is given to Christ, or in support of His cause, can never be given in vain. Thus given, the gift is an odour of a sweet-smelling savour, and shall in no wise lose its reward, though the end we have in view terminate in disappointment.

Mr. Crabb's perseverance ultimately overcame all difficulties. In the course of two years he collected £2,080, leaving £120 only to be paid in respect of the £2,200. Amongst those who contributed were his late Majesty King George IV., the Duke of York, the Duchess of Gloucester, the Duke of Kent, several of the Anglican Bishops, many of the nobility, and the Lord's people of every rank of life and every section of the Christian Church; but the principal part of the money was obtained from members of the Church of England, who are unquestionably more exempt from sectarian bigotry than any other portion of the Church of God. The remaining £120 was afterwards, upon an appeal being made to the people of Southampton, cheerfully contributed by them.

The chapel, when finished, was vested in trustees, upon perpetual trust, for the worship of God; but unconnected with any body of Dissenters. It is unnecessary to add, that neither Mr. Crabb nor any of his family acquired the slightest personal interest in the chapel, which is a standing monument of Mr. Crabb's zeal and energy of character, and serves to show what faith, under the blessing of God, can accomplish, in spite of opposition and difficulties apparently insurmountable.

CHAPTER XI.

Mr. Crabb's apostolic spirit.—His congregation.—His letter to
Lady —— upon Dr Wilson's acceptance of Holy Rhood church,
Southampton. — Kingsland school — Preaches on board the
Peninsular and Oriental Navigation Company's steamers.—His
labours amongst their seamen —His tract, addressed to the
sailors of Southampton.

MR CRABB was now a settled minister in Southampton,
but not being connected with any denominational section
of the Christian church he stood alone; and it was better
that he did, for his mind was of too wide a grasp to allow
him to be confined to one place, or circumscribed by settled
limits.   He was in the spiritual world what one of those
luminaries is amongst the heavenly bodies, which, having
no orbit, rolls along streaming with light, shedding a
mysterious influence far and wide, and is kept in an
untravelled path by the hand of Him who gave it existence,
and bids it shine.   He was endowed with an apostolic
spirit, and a love which embraced the ends of the earth.
As Nero wished that all mankind had but one head, he had
the same wish, — not, however, that he might destroy
the human family by cutting it off, but that he might be
enabled to preach the Gospel to every creature.   He had
a master-mind; and nothing was more true than what was
reproachfully said of him, " that he had set up for himself,"
with this limitation, however, that it was not in himself ·
but in Christ.   At one period of his life he was, I am

G

informed, offered ordination by Bishop Kaye, but declined
it, knowing that by joining the Establishment his hands
would be tied and his usefulness circumscribed.   As an
independent minister, the world was his parish—he could
preach by the way-side, in the fields, and in the lanes of
the cities and towns—he could go into any diocese in the
kingdom, even to the stronghold of Episcopal heresy,
" preaching the kingdom of God, and teaching those things
which concern the Lord Jesus Christ with all confidence,
no man forbidding him."   He desired nothing more than
to be a humble minister of Christ, ordained to that office
by the Holy Ghost, and sent by Him to be " the servant of
sinners, for Christ's sake ;" and in this character God
highly honoured him.

The congregation over which he now presided consisted
of many of those who had been brought to a knowledge of
the truth through his ministry, at the assembly-rooms
and elsewhere, and one of the galleries of the chapel was
filled by the sailors and fishermen who came over every
Sabbath from Itching Ferry.   Many respectable families
resident in Southampton, who were not attached to any
particular church, but loved the truth, knowing that they
should hear it from his lips, also attended his ministry ;
and as the Liturgy of the Church of England was introduced into the morning service (omitting some portions,
which, if always or periodically omitted in our church service
would be well for the sake of the minister and the feeble
and young of our congregations), many members of the
Church of England, finding no Gospel in the churches
where they and their fathers had been accustomed to
worship, attached themselves to his ministry.

It was not long after the erection of Mr. Crabb's
chapel, that a circumstance occurred which strikingly shows

his disinterested character and his earnest desire to promote the spiritual welfare of the people of Southampton.

The rector of the parish of Holy Rhood, in Southampton, who died in the year 1824, was a man who, however learned he may have been, preached little, if anything, of evangelical truth, and had by his lifeless ministry driven from the parish church most of those who prized and loved it. No sooner had it become known to Mr. Crabb that the appointment of his successor was vested in the Fellows of Queen's College, Oxford, and that the Rev. Dr. Wilson (the present esteemed rector of Holy Rhood), who held sound evangelical views, was likely to have an offer of the living, than he felt the importance of securing to Southampton the ministry of such a man, and accordingly he wrote to Dr. Wilson (to whom he was an entire stranger), setting forth the spiritual necessities of the town, and implored him to accept the living, and thus to help the cause of Christ. " Others," said he, " may be useful as Fellows of a College, but every one is not a faithful servant of Jesus Christ." He followed up this letter by others; but there is one dated 21st May, 1824, which shows so strikingly the spiritual state of Southampton, and the need at that time of a devoted minister in the church, that it is worthy of being noticed :

" 21st May, 1824.

"Rev and dear Sir,—In my haste, when writing my last letter, I forgot to name to you that in a town where nearly a thousand pounds can be got for a race-course in a few hours, we can get no society for the Jews, nor a missionary society for the conversion of the heathen, although we have a few gentlemen and ladies honoured by titles, but more by the religion of Jesus, who would gladly rally round the standard of the Gospel, if it were erected ; but the clergy—who are, in fact, the rulers of the people in Southampton—oppose these plans warmly as the chimera of the day. O my dear Sir, excuse me when I say, 'confer not with flesh and blood!' Souls are precious, and they are hastening to perdition. Pray hasten down to the camp in which the plague is spreading, and stand between your God and the people. I know that in the strength of God you will not want courage ; and He will be with you. O how I long to see the Church of England rise in piety and usefulness in this town ! Indeed, I fear that if an evangelical minister does not come to Holy Rhood, several pious church-people will leave the town.

"Did I know the objections which cause you to hesitate, though I am but the mouse compared with the lion, I would try and nibble away every particle of the net that would confine you to a College life."

Dr. Wilson eventually accepted the church of Holy Rhood ; and from that time it became crowded, and many who had been driven away to seek the evangelical ministry of dissenting chapels, returned to the church where their fathers had worshipped ; and many of Mr. Crabb's congregation also left him. But this was no more than he expected ; and he rejoiced in it, knowing that their places would be occupied by those who were perishing for lack of knowledge.

The deep interest which Mr. Crabb felt for the spiritual welfare of the people of Southampton was never more fully shown than in the trouble he took in this matter. The delight he felt upon Dr. Wilson's acceptance of the church of Holy Rhood, is thus expressed in a letter written by him to his kind friend Lady —— :

"Rumsey, 4th April, 1824.

"MY DEAR LADY ——,—Our dear Dr. Wilson opened his commission from the King of kings last Sabbath morning from, 'I say thou art Peter, and on this Rock,' &c. ; and in the evening, from 'We love Him, because He first loved us.' Most delightful sermons they were. Some hate him for his decided doctrine ; but many love him already ; and bless God for sending him. He will have two Gospel clergymen—one for Southampton and the other for Oakley. We have an Archdeacon Grace, from Ireland, coming to reside amongst us. He appears to be a man of God. What has God wrought for Southampton! We shall be strong in the Lord through these men of God. We shall now (in a future day) have a missionary society, and the dear Jews will be pleaded for by these good men, at whose feet I shall be glad to sit and pray for their success."

Mr. Crabb's exertions for the spiritual welfare of Kingsland have been already adverted to, but he saw little fruit from his labours there amongst the adult population, who had grown up and become hardened in iniquity. Having perused a book upon Infant Schools, he was determined to try what could be done amongst the young of that district, before they were contaminated by evil example, or hardened by a course of sin. He accordingly attempted the erection of a building in that locality, which should serve as a chapel and an infant school. His wishes upon this subject were thus expressed in a letter which he wrote to Dr. Lindoe :

"Southampton, 22nd September, 1825.

"MY DEAR DR. LINDOE,—Last night I met with your book on Infant Schools, and it arrested my attention until nearly midnight.

"I see the plan may be adopted and acted on in this wicked and depraved place (Kingsland) ; indeed, humanly speaking, I believe it is the only thing that can raise it. But unbelief says, 'How can it be accomplished ?'—and so it was said in relation to my labours at the Long-room, the building of my chapel, the establishing of the Penitentiary, &c., &c. ; and now the fearful are saying, 'But how will the chapel go on after I am dead ?' I am aware that if I engage in it and build, it will involve me in additional labour and responsibility ; but I need not fear if my heavenly Father smile upon me.

"My mind is so full of the subject that if I have but a little help, I shall, if my life be spared, begin the school and houses in a few weeks.

" There is only one thing I fear—lest my eye should not be single, or that I should have anything of vanity mingled with the plans. Oh, how I dread those feelings which would mar all before God ! May the eternal Spirit sanctify and keep my mind !"

Having determined to erect the school, he thus wrote to Lady —— :

" Perhaps I shall astonish you, when I tell you that having duly (I hope) considered the state of Kingsland-place and the adjoining places, I have fully made up my mind to erect an infant school there ; so that which was intended as a chapel and Sabbath-school, will be twice as large, or nearly so, with a large play-ground. This will cost nearly £500, perhaps more, and £100 per annum, to teach 200 children. I have begun collecting, and hope to be Divinely directed, then all will be well. I have consulted Drs. Wilson and Lindoe, and they both approve. Dr. Wilson will subscribe, and the dear Dr. Lindoe gave me, as he did for my chapel, the first £10, and an annual donation of one guinea, and Mrs. Lindoe £1 1s. per annum.

" Monday evening.—I have this day seen Miss Neave on the infant school ; she fears I shall have too much to do with pounds, shillings, and pence. I should indeed die in despair did not my Lord help, and promise still to help me."

Mr. Crabb having succeeded in erecting the school, it was publicly opened in the beginning of the year 1827. Every exertion was used to induce the people of Kingsland to send their children to it; and, as the instruction was almost gratuitous, it was soon filled. A Sabbath-school was also established ; and the room being convenient for the purpose, Divine service was performed in it, twice on the Lord's day and once in the week. A schoolmaster, who was able to preach, was engaged, and for many years he was a faithful labourer there under Mr. Crabb. Upon his resigning the situation, a valuable master was supplied by the Scripture Readers' Society, who allowed an annual sum of £30 towards his salary, which, by means of sub- scriptions obtained through Mr. Crabb, was increased to £70. This school is still in existence : but after the erection of schools in connection with the various new churches and chapels erected in the town, the number of its attendants fell off, and not more than seventy children are now receiving instruction ; the room is, however, still used for the promulgation of the Gospel on the Sabbath, and I am informed that the services are well attended by the people from the immediate neighbourhood.

The success which attended the school at Kingsland induced Mr Crabb to look out for further opportunities of instructing the rising generation amongst the working classes of Southampton. Having heard that six small tenements, at a place called Hill-life-land, which were held on lease for three lives, were to be sold for £250, he bought them, and built a school-house in the yard belong- ing to the tenements, at an expense of £90, where a num- ber of infant children, who were previously running wild in the neighbourhood without instruction, were taught, free of expense. The two lives having speedily dropped, Mr. Crabb, at the expense of £400, which he obtained by subscriptions, renewed the lease for three lives, which are still subsisting ; and the annual rent obtained for the tenements was, and still is, applied towards payment of the salary of the superintendent of the Kingsland school. The school which Mr. Crabb had established in this locality has, however, been discontinued.

We have now to follow Mr. Crabb in a new and important sphere of labour. In the year 1822, Southampton having become the place of rendezvous for the steamers of the Peninsular and Oriental Navigation Company, Mr. Crabb applied to Lieutenant Kendall, one of the Company's agents, and Mr. Lamb, their chief engineer, for permission to establish a religious service on shipboard, for the benefit of the sailors, who were destitute of all spiritual instruction, which they immediately gave; and Lieut. Kendall felt so much pleased with Mr. Crabb's proposal, that he volunteered to act as his clerk and give out the hymns. From this time Mr. Crabb commenced a weekly service on board one of the steamers, for the time being, in the harbour. The sailors at first did not seem disposed to attend; but the officers of many of the ships having required their crews to be present, they obeyed, and Mr. Crabb, who had the happy skill of winning the hearts of men, and overcoming evil with good, soon ingratiated himself into their favour, so that in a short time they heard him with interest, and brought their wives and children to his services.   Mr. Carlton, one of the managing Directors, being present at one of these services, was so struck with what he saw and heard, that, with a view to encourage the attendance of the men, he gave orders that on the days of service they might leave their work one hour before the usual time, thus preventing any infringement upon their time.

The success of these labours soon became apparent. Many of the seamen and their families were induced to become attendants upon public worship in the town; swearing was abated; the Bible was read, where before it had been neglected or unknown; children were placed under Christian instruction at the Sabbath-schools; and God was honoured where before He had been dishonoured.

It was my privilege, in the month of October, 1845, to

be present at one of these services, on board a large Oriental steamer. At the appointed hour of service, the large saloon having been made ready, the officers, with their friends and others who desired to be present, took their seats around the large dining-table; the rest of the saloon was filled with sailors, in their best attire, and many of them had brought with them their wives and children. The avenues and stairs leading to the saloon, and the decks above, where there was a possibility of hearing, were also crowded. Every sailor (except those who could not read — who were about one in twenty) had his Bible and Hymn-book. The service commenced with a hymn, which was followed by an appropriate and simple prayer. A chapter was then read from the word of God, another hymn followed, and then came the Sermon, in which Mr. Crabb set before his hearers the lost condition of man and his need of a Saviour; the love of Christ in dying in the sinner's place, and His readiness to save to the uttermost every one that came to Him; and this he did with such happy illustrations, drawn from subjects familiar to seamen, such earnestness of manner, such touching appeals to the conscience, and such affectionate beseechings and winning touches of pathos, as drew tears from many. I saw the captain and many of the sailors weep; for they felt that he was in earnest, and that they ought to be in earnest too.

In those days scarcely a ship belonging to the Oriental and Peninsular Company left the port of Southampton until Mr. Crabb had preached to her crew, and every ship was well supplied with Bibles and Prayer-books. It was very different, however, with the West India Steam Navigation Company, who would not allow any preaching on board their vessels, nor give any countenance to the spiritual instruction of their seamen. They did not hesitate to clear their ships on the Sabbath ; but this the Peninsular and Oriental Company never did, except under very pressing circumstances. It is not my province to draw a distinction between the crews of the ships of the one Company and the other : but I believe it is well known that there was a vast difference between them.

Such was Mr. Crabb's desire to do good to these men, that he was not satisfied with merely preaching on shipboard, but printed a letter which he addressed to them, under the title of " An Affectionate Letter to the Seamen belonging to the Oriental and Peninsular Steam Navigation Company, and the South Western Steam Navigation Company, and the other Seamen belonging to the Port of Southampton ;" 2,000 copies of which were distributed gratuitously. It was a most useful tract, and consisted of the following heads :—1. Resolve to do the whole of your duty on board ship with the cheerfulness of honest and upright men. 2. Never indulge in vicious conversation. 3. Resist all inducements to profane swearing. 4. Reject, with abhorrence, all temptations to tell a lie. 5. Forsake at once and for ever, and with manly indignation, all persuasions to drunkenness. 6. The long experience I have had in observing what has happened to seamen, induces me to caution you against smuggling. 7. Most affectionately do I urge you all to possess a Bible, and as often as you can, in the time allotted to you, *read that Bible.* 8. Live in the daily practice of private prayer. 9. Trust in Christ for salvation. He then pointed out, under various heads, the advantages of religion ; each head being filled up by forcible remarks and interesting anecdotes, and it concluded with a form of prayer for a sailor. But Mr. Crabb did not stop here. Having read an interesting sermon, preached on the death of Richard Weeks, of Great Missenden, Bucks, he (with the permission of the author) printed 2,000 copies at his own expense, and distributed them amongst the sailors of Southampton. He also compiled and published a collection of Hymns for Seamen, which was gratuitously distributed amongst them. These labours of Mr Crabb were duly appreciated by the Directors of the Oriental and Peninsular Company, and they kindly sent him £25, towards defraying his printing expenses.

These days, however, have passed away. There are now no services on board any of these ships. The voice of praise once heard in Southampton harbour, no longer

> "When twilight meek upon the palpitating breast
> Of ocean melts in rosy calm away,"

sends its echoes over its silent waters, " in deep-toned chants and melodies divine;" the sound of prayer is hushed, the standard of truth is no longer unfurled; and he who stood upon the deck of yonder gallant ship, as an ambassador of the King of kings, to proclaim His message of love, has been called away to give account of what he did, and, alas! to bear witness against those who rejected him.

CHAPTER XII.

Mr. Crabb's next labours — and which brought him
more into public notice than any of those which preceded
them—had relation to a race of people who were then, as
they still are, outcasts and aliens from society, dwelling as
heathens in a Christian land — and these were the gipsies.
The origin of these people, upon which so many opinions
have been hazarded, it is not my purpose to discuss. It
is enough for us to know that those who dwell amongst
us are Englishmen—having souls to be saved, and for
whom there is redemption through the blood of Christ.

The circumstances under which Mr. Crabb's attention
was first directed to this interesting people made a deep
impression upon him. During the Winchester assizes
of 1827, having occasion to speak to the Rev. Henry
Thompson, the sheriff's chaplain, he went into the
Criminal Court for that purpose. As he entered, the
judge was, acording to the Draconic code of that day,
passing sentence of death on two criminals; to one of

whom he held out the hope of mercy, but to the other of
whom, a poor gipsy, who was convicted of horse-stealing,
he said no hope could be given.   "The young man," says
Mr. Crabb, "for he was but a youth, immediately fell on
his knees, and with uplifted hands and eyes, apparently
unconscious of any person being present but the judge
and himself, addressed him as follows : ' Oh! my Lord,
save my life !'   The judge replied, ' No : you can have no
mercy in this world; I and my brother judges have come
to the determination to execute horse-stealers, especially
gipsies, because of the increase of the crime.'   The sup-
pliant, still on his knees, entreated—' Do, my Lord Judge,
save my life !—do, for God's sake, for my wife's sake, for
my baby's sake !'   ' No,' replied the Judge, 'I cannot :
you should have thought of your wife and child before.'
He then ordered him to be taken away, and he was
literally dragged from his earthly judge."

Mr. Crabb on leaving the court, found on the outside,
seated upon the ground, an old woman, and a very young
one, the wife of the condemned criminal.   There were two
children with them—the eldest three years, and the other
an infant, *fourteen days* old, which the old woman was
holding in her arms whilst she endeavoured to comfort
its weeping mother.   Mr. Crabb sought to improve
the event by speaking to them of the evils of sin, and
its inevitable results both in this world and that which
is to come.   The scene he had witnessed in the court made
a deep impression on his mind; and having read Hoyland's
" Survey of the Gipsies," he felt an earnest desire to make
some attempt to promote the spiritual improvement of these
unhappy beings.   The more he contemplated their condition, the more they appeared to him to be worthy of deep
commiseration ; and although he felt the difficulties which

attended any endeavours which might be made on their behalf, he was satisfied that their case, though full of discouragements, was by no means hopeless. An opportunity of beginning this work soon presented itself, and he quickly availed himself of it. A few weeks after he was at Winchester, he met the old woman whom he had seen there, and he invited her and her daughter-in-law (the widow of the condemned gipsy, who had in the interval been executed,) to call at his house at Spring-hill, which they accordingly did; and the result of this visit was, that they consented to place a granddaughter of the old woman (the child of another daughter, whose husband had been transported,) and the elder child of the widow, with Mr. Crabb, in order that he might place them under training and instruction. In a few days the two children, one aged six and the other three years, were accordingly given over to his care. Having kept them in his house during three days, that they might be initiated in the habits of civilized life, he put them in his infant school, where they were brought into discipline and taught to read. The gipsy women being satisfied with what Mr. Crabb was doing for the children, in a short time induced some of their acquaintance to entrust to him three other gipsy children, who were also placed in the school. The efforts to instruct these children having proved successful, Mr. Crabb began to devise some plan by which, under the Divine blessing, these outcasts of the human family, for whose souls no man seemed to care, might be effectually and permanently benefited. Being unable, however, by means of his own, to accomplish this benevolent design, he opened his mind upon the subject to the Rev. Dr. Wilson, the Incumbent of Holy Rhood, and Sir Matthew Blakeston, Captain Davis, R.N., Mr. Owen Lloyd, Mr.

N. Cousins, and Mr. Mayor—gentlemen of high Christian character, then resident in Southampton ; who, after some prayerful consideration of the subject, entered into Mr. Crabb's views, and shortly afterwards formed themselves into a Committee, "for taking into consideration the condition of the Gipsy race, and devising some means for their moral and spiritual improvement." The Committee met together for the first time on the 12th of November, 1827 , and with a view to procure such information as might throw light on the character and habits of the gipsy tribe, and aid them to proceed safely and wisely in their undertaking, they drew up a paper—copies of which were sent to the Editors of the " Christian Guardian " and " Christian Observer," the Secretary of the Home Missionary Society, and various persons who had either written on the subject of the Gipsies, or had interested themselves on their behalf—requesting information and suggestions as to the best means of promoting their religious and general improvement These circulars brought out many curious and interesting particulars as to the condition, habits, and character of these people, much of which will be found in Mr. Crabb's publication, called "The Gipsies' Advocate." The reply of the Rev. Charles Hyatt, the Secretary of the Home Missionary Society, to the inquiries made of him, contains so much interesting information, that I am induced to think it may, even at the present time, be read with interest if not with profit .

" My attention," he says, " was first called to the gipsies in the year 1820, by a letter addressed to the Committee of the Home Missionary Society, by a lady of the name of Gladwell, of Bath (I believe she is a member of the Society of Friends), entreating the Committee to take under their immediate consideration the state of that unhappy people In the Committee there was strong prejudice in many minds against any attempt ,

and, I am ashamed to say, I took that side of the question
most warmly. At length the Committee came to a resolution
of sending out two persons on a tour into Cambridgeshire,
Northamptonshire, Bedfordshire, &c., to ascertain from an actual
survey what was the state and condition of the gipsies in those
counties ; and having determined to select two of opposite opinions from the Committee, I had the (which I now consider)
honour to be selected, with a warm friend to the cause, for the
journey. My coolness in the cause was considered necessary
to counterbalance any exaggerated statement from my more
enthusiastic companion. Permit me to add, that if I went out
rather unfriendly to the cause deputed to me by the Committee,
I am happy to tell you and your worthy coadjutors that I did
not return in that spirit, but felt all the enthusiasm of my more
sanguine companion ; and from that day to this, and I hope to
my dying day, shall feel a lively interest in anything likely to
promote the welfare of 18,000 human beings in this highly-
favoured country, as destitute of moral and religious advantages as was Africa thirty years past. But I am sorry to
inform you, what no doubt you have observed, or what perseverance in this good cause will lead you to observe, that but
' few seem to care for their state ;' and I shall never forget an
important remark of the late excellent Legh Richmond, with
whom I spent a day at Turvey, on the gipsy business. ' Ah,
sir,' said that worthy man, ' the scene of distress you describe
is too near home. If you could prove to British Christians
that 18,000 beings were in the state you represent the gipsies
in, at the most distant part of the globe, you would soon find
funds and missionaries enough to send to them the word of
eternal life.' I have found his remark quite correct. Englishmen are fond of looking to the ends of the earth, and in so
doing overlook home. I rejoice in our missionary spirit, and
with my humble abilities I have encouraged it; but I am
sorry that home (especially the poor gipsies,) is lost sight of.
But, my dear sir, I trust you will not think these remarks
designed to check your zeal and that of the worthy gentlemen
with whom you are engaged. On the contrary, it is with a
design to encourage you and them ; and I still think that
British philanthropists only want the matter presented to

them in a tangible shape, and they will embark in it. The Lord grant you may be the honoured instrument of directing attention to it!

"In reply to your 1st Query—'What has been done for the moral and religious, &c.?' Nothing that I am aware of, on a general plan. The attention of the religious public was called to their unhappy state by several letters which appeared in the 'Christian Observer,' in 1808 and 1809 ; and since then a few remarks in the 'Evangelical Magazine,' and especially in the 'Home Missionary Magazine' for 1820, 1821, &c., but no plan devised or society formed ; but the most interesting publication I have seen, is a work published by John Hoyland, of Northampton (a member of the Society of Friends). I doubt not but you have seen the work ; if not, I hope you will not lose a day in obtaining it.

"Query 2nd—'In case of failure of any plan,' &c. As before observed, I am not aware of any organized plan—nothing but attempts by individuals. These have not succeeded in doing good to any extent ; yet, to my certain knowledge, some good has arisen out of these : a family of the name of Smith, of Cambridge, became very decidedly pious, and received the sacrament of the Lord's supper from the Rev. Mr. Simeon, of that town, whose curate wrote me, in answer to an inquiry, that he did not know a more pious woman in all the congregation : all their children have been educated in Mr. Simeon's Sunday-school. Another woman I met in Bedfordshire, gave evident proof of her conversion to Christianity ; but still, these are partial instances. I need not inform you, that persecutions and prosecution have all failed, and I trust the friends at Southampton will never use these. I think that the good people that have commenced instructing, have not persevered in the cause, but have been too sanguine ; and not reaping expected fruits, have given over. But who that knows human nature and the state of the gipsies, can expect fruit at once ?—they must 'continue in well doing.'

"3rd—'What do you recommend, &c.?' This, sir, is an interesting question, and I am sorry that I cannot answer it in any possible way to my own satisfaction, and, I fear, not to yours. Of the old wandering parents, but little I think can be done, more than benevolent and pious Christians visiting their tents, when in your neighbourhood, and reading the word of God to them ; conversing with them on the loss they sustain in the want of knowing how to read, and mingling with other persons ; and permit me to say, that if females of a little respectability in life can be prevailed on to visit them, they may depend that all their fears of being insulted will soon vanish : the gipsies will treat them with great respect. But the children must be the great object of Christian attention. I cannot help thinking that if a school to receive and educate them was established, and after being educated they were put out as apprentices to a trade, this would be the likeliest way of effectually benefiting them. In this plan the Society of Friends, and Church of England, and all Dissenters would unite. But the expense would be very great ; and another difficulty is—I always find the gipsies not willing to part with their children : they are generally fond of the old and the young.

"Wishing you all perseverance, without which nothing can or will be done in so good a cause,

"I am, &c.,

"Charles Hyatt."

Mr. John Hoyland, the author of the " Survey of the Gipsies," in a letter written by him to the Committee, told them :

"In my apprehension it almost amounts to demonstration, that nothing short of domestication of their children will be found sufficient to counteract their desultory habits. I derive peculiar satisfaction from the idea that infant schools are admirably adapted to facilitate this object ; and also that your attempt has not commenced on a larger scale, which might have rendered success more difficult and doubtful, and its magnitude have deterred other parts of the nation from following your example."

The following letters,—one written by direction of the Rev. Rowland Hill, and the other written by the Rev. Charles Simeon,—will serve to show how little sympathy was at that time felt by the best men for the gipsies, and how generally (for most persons thought as these two men of God did) it was considered that nothing could be done for their spiritual welfare :

" London, 24th November, 1827.

"I am directed by Mr. Hill, whose eyes and strength are so much impaired by age, to inform you that he is obliged to resign all his active attention to many charities, in which he was formerly engaged. Mr. Hill knows nothing of those roving tribes called gipsies, but generally supposed them to be an idle, worthless set of wanderers, that are a reproach to the police of the country, and ought first to be brought under the cognizance of the civil magistrate, before any effectual means can be provided for their religious improvement, or future spiritual good. Mr. Hill may have been misinformed about this race of vagabonds ; but with him an increase of rest, and not of active exertions, is naturally required.

" I am, Sir, &c.,

" ———— ————."

I may observe, that the Rev. Charles Simeon had been written to in consequence of the statement made in Mr. Hyatt's letter, that he had been the means of leading a female gipsy to the Saviour of sinners:

" What," he says, "can be done for such a wandering tribe, I know not. What place will allow you to congregate them ? And how can you fix them ? It is only by circulating tracts among them that you can do them good. The Government must first *fix* them. Then you may hope to do them good.

" K. C., Cambridge, November 25th, 1827.

The Committee were not discouraged by these letters; but some time elapsed before they determined upon any fixed plan of operations. They did not, however, remain inactive, nor was Mr. Crabb likely to rest satisfied with deliberation without endeavour. It having been ascertained that a number of gipsies were in the habit of encamping on Shirley Common, and other places near

Southampton, the Committee entered into an engagement with a man of Christian character well acquainted with the gipsies, and capable of imparting instruction to infants and adults, to visit their encampments; and the result of this movement was, that in about a year and a half twenty adults and children had been brought by the Committee under moral and religious instruction.   Six women of the number were induced to take up their residence at Southampton, and were employed in such work as they were found most capable of undertaking, with a view to assist in supporting their families, and diminish the expenses incurred in defraying their rent, and in clothing them.   Four boys were apprenticed to different trades, and the younger children placed at school.   It was a leading object in every arrangement to endeavour *gradually* to overcome their early, deep-rooted habits of restlessness, sloth, and inactivity, and the evils arising from *gratuitous* charity, by stimulating them to industrious and provident habits, and inducing them to contribute small weekly deposits out of their earnings for their future maintenance and clothing; thus raising the tone of *self-exertion*, and giving suitable encouragement when their personal efforts entitled them to some testimony of approbation.

A tolerably correct estimate was formed of the character of the individuals thus brought under what might be fairly termed civilization, and of the success likely to attend the efforts thus made by means of frequent visitation amongst them; and the Committee were encouraged by what they saw, to continue their labours.

Such was the commencement of this work in which Mr. Crabb took an active and leading part, and to which he devoted much of his time and energies.   By his exertions money was obtained for carrying it on, and many persons of Christian character were induced to give it their support. The operations of the Committee were however at this period of a private kind; but having at the end of five years found it practicable to continue their operations on a larger scale, they issued a report of what they had done, from which it appeared that forty-six gipsies had been brought out of their vagrant and predatory habits of life to a settled state of domiciliation in the town and neighbourhood of Southampton; and with a view to promote the object in which they were engaged, the Committee suggested, that if committees were formed in other towns and places throughout the kingdom and a suitable person were employed under each committee as a missionary to visit the gipsy tents, and give them instruction, much good might (looking at what had been done at Southampton) be reasonably anticipated, especially if the members of the Committee were themselves active in the work, and obtained assistance and support from ministers of the Gospel. I am not aware that these suggestions of the Southampton Committee were acted upon by any of the men of God living in London, or any of the provinces; though had the appeal been made on behalf of the gipsies in parts beyond the seas, the subject might have been taken up, and probably a Society upon a large scale would by this time have been in existence.

· Notwithstanding the many discouragements to which the Southampton Committee were exposed, they went on steadily in their operations. Mr. Crabb, however, was not content that their labours should be confined to Southampton : he longed for a wider sphere of usefulness ; and with a view to more extensive operations, in the month of May, 1831, he visited the Epsom race-course, in the expectation of meeting a large company of gipsies, who generally attended the races, from whom he hoped to obtain some tidings of those who travelled through the midland counties, numbers of whom resided during the winter months in London. Stanley, the Southampton Scripture-reader to the gipsies, was sent to acquaint them with Mr. Crabb's intention to visit them; and he was introduced to great numbers, of whom till then he had not the least knowledge. One of the men,—a relative of Stanley, whom he had never before seen,—introduced him to the different families as the person employed by the Committee at Southampton to impart religious instruction to the gipsies; and upon Mr. Crabb's arrival at Epsom, he was introduced to them by Stanley and his kind relative, as "the gentleman, the gipsies' friend, from Southampton." "I am come," said Mr. Crabb, "nearly a hundred miles to see you; do you not, therefore, think that I love you?" Many of them said, "Yes, sir." "Come, then," said he, "make room for me in one of your tents; for I must sit down with you, and tell you the way to heaven." A little wash-tub was fixed, with the bottom upwards, and covered with one of their shawls, for him to sit on; and having by his kind and conciliatory manner engaged their attention, he made them acquainted with the designs which were then in contemplation for their social and spiritual improvement, and exhorted them to avail themselves of the opportunities which might be presented to them; assuring them that those who were engaged in the work, had no other motive than to do them good. Having pressed the subject upon them, by pointing out the miseries to which they and their children were exposed, by their unsettled habits of life, he set before them the truths of revelation; and having exhorted them to read the word of God, and distributed a few tracts and books amongst them, he left them apparently much impressed with what they had heard.

The efforts of the Southampton Committee were now beginning to be known amongst the gipsy tribe in all parts of the kingdom. In truth, these efforts were more extensively known amongst them than amongst Christian men in general; and as it was important that a greater interest should be excited both amongst the gipsies themselves and the friends of missions, Mr. Crabb established an annual meeting at his house and grounds at Spring-hill, Southampton, to which he invited the reformed gipsies and their families, and such others of their tribe as were disposed to hear what had been, and was designed to be done for the improvement of their race. The first annual meeting was held in the month of December, 1829, and it was very numerously attended by the gentry from the neighbourhood of Southampton; and every subsequent annual meeting was more largely attended by persons from London and various parts of the country, who appeared to take great interest in the proceedings.

At each return of the anniversary crowds of gipsies came into Southampton from all parts of the country with caravans, carts, and rude vehicles, driven by broken-down horses, ponies, and donkeys; and, at an early hour, they might be seen in long procession winding up the hill to Mr. Crabb's residence. As they arrived, they were admitted into the field adjoining the house, where a camp, consisting generally of about 150 persons, was formed previously to the meeting.

The annual meeting was always of an interesting and instructive character. It was opened with a hymn, after which Mr. Crabb prayed, and read a portion of Scripture. He then gave the gipsies an address, in which he set before them the evils of sin, especially of pilfering and fortune-telling,—the advantages of industry and the blessings of social life. He compared the state of those who were leading a vagabond life and those who had been placed under instruction, and were now gaining a livelihood by their honest labours, and exhorted them to avail themselves of the advantages set before them. In these addresses he preached to them Jesus, set before them the mercy of God in Him, the fulness and freeness of that mercy, the resurrection of the dead, the solemnities of the judgment, the consequent danger of slighting the Gospel, and the blessed privileges and prospects of those who fled for refuge to Christ. No man was better qualified to address such a class of people as he was—for he knew the secrets of their tents, the habits of their lives, and the peculiarities which attached to them; but he took care (as an eminently Christian gipsy, one of his converts, told me) to preach not only to the gipsies, but to the fine ladies and gentlemen who were present, and who, if they had bestowed one half of what they expended in vanity, in helping the gipsy cause, might have enabled the Committee to establish a mission throughout the length and breadth of the land.

After the address, letters were read from persons resident in various parts of the kingdom who were interested in the gipsy cause; and as these letters generally contained some interesting particulars, he never failed to accompany them by some useful practical remarks. The service then concluded with the Doxology. The school-room being cleared, the tables were prepared for the dinner,—which, on these occasions, was provided for the gipsies; and during the interval those of the visitors who desired to obtain information from them as to their circumstances and prospects had an opportunity of doing so. Dinner being announced, the tables, which were spread with a profusion of roast and boiled beef, vegetables, and plum pudding, were soon occupied by Mr. Crabb's swarthy guests, who, on this one day of the year, obtained a taste of the comforts of civilized life, and had an opportunity of contrasting its blessings with the miseries of a houseless, homeless, wandering life. Few parties in the country were better waited upon, or had more honourable servants, Mr. Crabb himself and his two sons being assisted in that office by a large number of the visitors, who, "stripped of conventional deceptions, untrammelled from the harness of society," by thus "condescending to men of low estate," and imitating Him who amongst His disciples was "as one that serveth," recommended the gospel which had been proclaimed to them, and awakened in their hearts feelings of gratitude which had never before been called forth by similar demonstrations of kindness towards them. Dinner being finished, and thanks returned to Almighty God, a distribution of blankets and warm clothing was made amongst those who stood in need of them, and those who were without Bibles were supplied with them.

It is a remarkable fact, that most of the gipsies had no idea of a future state of existence, and wondered, as they of old, "what it should mean." In this respect they are worse than most of the remaining heathen nations and tribes, there being few who have not at least some traditional notion of a future state. Mr. Crabb therefore pressed this doctrine upon them, as likely to lead them to further inquiry, and an investigation of Scripture truth. This doctrine—Christ and the resurrection—so alarming to the impenitent and so cheering to the Christian, seems, in the present day, to be much lost sight of in the Christian

ministry. The great hope of the church is doubtless the
glorious appearing of Christ; but the resurrection, when
this mortal shall put on immortality, and this corruptible
shall put on incorruption, is a fundamental doctrine in-
volving, as the apostle tells us, the most momentous
truths; for if there be no resurrection, "Christ himself
is not risen;" "all preaching is vain," "faith is vain,"
the "ministers of Christ are false witnesses," we are "yet
in our sins," and all those dear to us who "have fallen
asleep in Christ are perished;" and no subject, connected as it is with the final destiny of man, is more
calculated to arouse the impenitent and unbelieving. In
reference to this doctrine, how unsurpassably grand is the
following passage from an American divine:—"No doctrine," he says, "devised by philosophy concerning man is
so sublime or so fitted to furnish consolation and hope to
beings whose life in this world is a moment, and whose
end is the grave. To that dark and desolate habitation
man, by the twilight of nature, looks forward in despair
as his final home. All who have gone before him have
pointed their feet to its silent chambers, and not one has
returned to announce that an opening has been discovered
to a more lightsome and desirable region. His own feet
tread the same melancholy path. As he draws nigh no
lamp illumes the darkness within,—no crevice opens to
the eye a glimpse of the regions which lie beyond. Philosophy has no consolation for herself, and can administer
none to him. 'Here,' she coldly and suddenly cries, 'is
the end of man. From nothing he sprang, to nothing he
returns. All that remains of him is the dust, which here
mingles with its native earth.' But revelation approaches,
and exclaims, 'Lazarus, come forth!' In a moment the
earth heaves, the tomb uncloses, and a form bright as the

sun, and arrayed in immortality, rises from the earth, and stretching its wings towards heaven, escapes from the astonished sight."—*Dwight, Vol. V.*, 437.

The anniversary meetings held by Mr. Crabb were productive of much good, by breaking down the prejudices of the gipsies, and leading them to discover that those whom they had formerly looked upon with suspicion were their true friends. Those of them whose children had been placed at school had an opportunity of seeing the advantages which had accrued to them from the instruction they had received; and as several of them had been placed out to trades, or other occupations in the town, those advantages were the more apparent. These meetings, moreover, had the effect of stirring up other Christian men to "go and do likewise." The Rev. John West, rector of Chettle, in Dorsetshire, was so struck with what he saw at the first anniversary, that in order to test the practicability of carrying out the plans of the Southampton Committee in his own parish, he erected two cottages, in each of which he placed a gipsy family; and that they might be kept from idle habits, and help to maintain their children, whom he placed under instruction in his parochial school, he allotted to each family an acre of ground for cultivation. Similar efforts were made by Christian men in various parts of England and Scotland, the results of which gave great encouragement to those by whom they were made. Great difficulty, however, soon arose in placing the gipsy children in the parochial schools, the townspeople objecting, and not without reason, to the association of their children with those of the gipsies. Mr. West felt the force of the objection, and suggested to Mr. Crabb the importance of having a school for gipsy children exclusively; a suggestion which was immediately embraced by Mr. Crabb, as a beginning at the right end. Mr. West forthwith issued a short publication, entitled "A Plea for Educating the Children of the Gipsies," dedicated to Lord Ashley, and addressed to the nobility, gentry, and magistrates of the county of Dorset, in which he urged the formation of an institution for the maintenance and education of at least twenty-four orphan gipsy children, under six years of age; or boys and girls, not older, from the largest and most destitute gipsy families. The subject was soon taken up by many of the clergy, and by persons of influence in the counties of Dorset and Hampshire, amongst whom were the Rev. Dr. Marsh and the Rev. C. B. Coney, of Kimmeridge. An appeal having been issued by those two gentlemen, in conjunction with Mr. Crabb, on behalf of the proposed institution, a sum of about £1,200 was soon subscribed, of which £100 were given by the Committee of Council of Education, by whom the object was justly regarded as one in which the country itself was interested. A suitable site having, through the liberality of Francis Archibald Stuart, Esq., been obtained at Farnham, near Blandford, on the 24th of July, 1845, the first stone of the Gipsy Asylum and Industrial School was laid. A large assemblage was gathered together to witness the ceremony, amongst whom were many of the gipsy people, who looked on with wonder at so novel a movement on their behalf. The foundation-stone was not laid by one of the great or rich, but by one of the meanest and poorest—as regards this world—present at that assembly; and he was an aged and reformed gipsy. Previously to the ceremony, with great simplicity and deep emotion, he said:

"Kind friends, ladies and gentlemen, I am come here as a true gipsy, to take part in this good work; and I will do it as well as I can, if not so well as I could wish. My father died many years ago, but some time before he went out of this life he cursed God, and from that time he never had any rest. He was attended by a doctor, and what I have told you was the cause of his weeping to the day of his death; he could not rest, but I hope, through God's mercy, he repented. We children would often catch him weeping, and we would ask him what he cried for; but he would say that we could not understand, and tell us never to curse the Lord. This is the true account of my father, who is dead and gone. I acknowledge that I have been a very wicked man almost all my life, but I hope the time came for me to alter. I am come here, in sincerity of heart, to lay the foundation-stone for the good of the poor gipsy children, and I hope the building will be raised, and that the work will stand till the end of the world. I hope the gipsy parents will place their children here willingly, under the care of the good Christian gentlemen and ladies. I have no more to say, only I hope that God will bless our Queen and all the Royal Family, and all the good Christians who support this school."

The trowel was then handed to the old gipsy by the architect, and he went to work in good earnest, spreading the mortar profusely, and some coins of the present reign having been duly placed, laid the stone, adjusted it with the plumbing-line, and struck it thrice with the mallet, amidst the hearty cheers of the spectators. He then, amidst much applause, said, — "May God Almighty's blessing rest upon this work! May the gentlemen who proposed it be blessed, and all who support it! God bless the Queen, Prince Albert, and all the Royal Family!"

Mr. Crabb's speech on that occasion was no less striking than interesting:

"My dear friends," he said, "we have, by God's blessing, commenced a good work, but we have not yet done praying for the gipsies on this occasion, for, although my worthy friend, the Rector of this parish, is the leading projector of this school, he does not know the whole of my gipsy plans. I have in my hand a prayer, by a gipsy woman, who wished it to be put under the foundation-stone; but we will not bury a prayer under a stone, if we do this with money. Let us all, then, join in this prayer which I will read, just as it was written from the dictation of the Christianised gipsy woman." He then read as follows :

"Oh, thou great Searcher of Hearts, hear the prayer of an unworthy worm. Grant that this plan that Thy dear servants have undertaken in the behalf of the dear wandering tribes, may prosper in their hands. Incline the hearts of the parents to give up their dear offspring into the hands of those dear and kind friends that feel this great interest in the salvation of their souls. Grant, O most merciful Lord, that their parents may give them up as Hannah did her dear son Samuel. O Lord, hear and answer the prayers of the unworthiest widow, in the behalf of this laudable object, and sanctify the spot, that many thousands of the rising generations may be born again on this spot; and may the Lord, for the sake of His dear Son, doubly reward the kind hearts, for undertaking this great work; and may the Lord God sanctify both people and preachers, and grant that this may turn out to the furtherance of this blessed cause, to the glory of His holy name, that souls may be saved, and Thy dear servants' hearts may be satisfied in seeing souls brought to Himself."

Mr. Crabb continued :—"I could not have discharged

my conscience, nor the trust imposed upon me, without
reading this prayer, in which you have no doubt joined;
and I hope that God will hear and answer this prayer,
which this poor gipsy widow has put up in behalf of her
tribe, and of all who wish to do them spiritual as well as
temporal good. It is remarkable, in the case of this
reclaimed woman, that the cause of bringing the gipsies
to Christianity has prospered most in her particular clan
I need hardly say, after having laboured for a long period
in Southampton and the neighbourhood, to reclaim gipsies,
and not without success, that I am greatly rejoiced that I
have been permitted to live to see this day—a day most
remarkable and glorious. I am truly happy that the
cause of converting and civilizing the gipsies has been
taken up, and so warmly, by my worthy friend, the Rev
John West. Whatever good I may, through the Divine
blessing, have been able to effect among this singular but
interesting' people — the suggestion of a school for the
training and care of the orphan and other children of the
gipsies—the only course that can be permanently successful was Mr. West's first plan; and while we give what is
due to this excellent clergyman and his worthy coadjutors,
to God be all the glory. No one could be better calculated to take up the cause of the poor gipsies than Mr.
West, for he has been in the Hudson's Bay Company's
territories, as Chaplain to the Company, and Missionary to
the North West American Indians. In the year 1821 he
pitched a Gospel-tent at the Red River Settlement, which
has been the means of bringing many a wandering Indian
to the feet of the Saviour. Mr. West met with people in
the dreary wilds of that part of the world, whose wandering habits of life very much resembled our gipsies, and
therefore he is peculiarly adapted for the work he has

undertaken. From what he has seen in his labours abroad, and from his general knowledge of mankind, he is aware that nothing permanently good can be done unless the children are instructed. The great evil in the gipsies, and bar to their conversion, is their wicked practice of fortune-telling, particularly among young women and girls; there are a great many now present, but I hope none who encourage this wicked abomination, which leads to a train of evils but little considered. What is it, but a 'refuge of lies' and deceit, the encouragement of which tends to undermine religious faith, and to peril the immortal soul. Oh, dear young ladies present, never encourage fortune-telling. Now, the poor gipsy children, if instructed and trained up in the nurture and admonition of the Lord, will, as many other children have, be instruments in the hands of God in the conversion of their parents. A little instructed child will say, 'Daddy, why do you swear? my teacher tells me it is wicked to swear.' Or, 'Mammy, why do you tell a lie? my teacher says the Lord hates a lie and will punish all liars.' Now, these and such like are words of great effect and power, for, as you know, the little ones cannot be got rid of: they are like nails driven into planks of oak—you know what I mean, they are pretty firm in such timber. If we were about to build a palace, what interest would be taken in laying the foundation-stone; but we are about to build something far beyond a palace; for palaces, with all such things in this world, shall pass away, whilst our humble building, which we commence in faith and hope, will last, if not in its earthly materials, in its effects, to all eternity. Let us only build in faith, and God will love and bless his servants who commence such works in faith and hope. As to the tale told by Charles, the aged gipsy, he has not told the whole story about his father. As might be supposed, he feels this matter deeply, and I can tell you there is this about gipsies which he did not like to state,—they never desert their aged parents; such is their dutiful affection, that if their parents get old and too infirm to walk, the children carry them about from place to place, and never leave them till they are no more, and their bodies have been decently interred. There are many fine feelings about the despised gipsies, which it would be well for many who call themselves Christians to imitate. But to return to the poor old departed gipsy, the father of Charles; his history will be found in a tract called " The Dying Gipsy," which can be bought at Blandford, or any other town in the kingdom, and will be found well worth reading. I will not enter into the particulars of this history, further than to say, that he gave a guinea to a person to read the Scriptures to him. This was a large sum, which I do not think any person ought to have taken for such a purpose; he also gave a reward for some one to pray for him; and he said that all the long years he had lived no one had said a word to him about his soul, or about the Gospel of Christ. Was it any wonder, then, that the gipsies were so dark, when, although they were wandering about in a Christian country, no one cared about their souls ? Such, however, is not the case now, for clergymen and ladies, as well as other pious persons, will go into their tents and read the Word of God to them. Then look at the annals of our prisons. Some time ago there were many gipsies tried, but it is not so now, as it is a rare thing to find a gipsy committed to prison for crime. I will relate to you an instance of what occurred some time since. A gipsy at Southampton was committed for coming, but he learned this on board the hulks ! Yes ; he had

been previously transported, and when on board the hulks
for punishment and reformation, he got the apparatus and
learned the art of making counterfeit coin ! The farmers
about here are much prejudiced against the gipsies. I
have heard that some in this neighbourhood are thinking
my friend, Mr. West, is bringing a nuisance into the
neighbourhood; but such, I can assure them, will not be
the case, as gipsies are not nuisances to any neighbourhood, if they are treated with kindness and Christian
forbearance. I know a lady in Hampshire who always
employs gipsies to watch her hop-grounds, and they are
trusty watchmen and good servants. If people will treat
them kindly, they are very accessible, and will attend to
what is said for their instruction and good. I have lately
seen an account of a tribe of gipsies in the neighbourhood
of Taunton who attend church, and are most attentive and
orderly in their devotions. My good friends, again I say
that I rejoice to see this day; and I am most happy to
see here so very large and so respectable an attendance
on this blessed occasion ; for, considering the prejudice
abroad, I did not expect to see so many. I have been
long labouring in this cause, almost alone, at one time it
cost me at least £100 a year, and I have been asked why
I continued to go on with this object ? My answer was,
that I had set my hand to the plough, and, by God's
assistance, did not intend to look back. My good friend,
the Rector of this parish, has come forward, with other
Christian people, and the Lord has already much blessed
their exertions, and He will, no doubt, continue His blessing. I could tell you many instances of the conversion of
gipsies to Christianity, who have brought up their children
in the right way. The daughter of one, who suffered
under that most dreadful malady—cancer of the breast,—

was a magnificent Christian; and when she was under-going a painful operation, which happened on the very day that the negroes of the West Indies were set free from slavery, in the midst of her agony, on remembering the circumstance, such was her feeling for her fellow-creatures, that she exclaimed, 'This is a glorious day for the negroes: God grant His blessing upon it.' I will conclude by say-ing, this is a glorious day for the gipsies; may God, for Christ's sake, grant His abundant blessing upon this work and labour of love in which we are now engaged!"

This speech will serve to show the largeness of Mr. Crabb's benevolence, and how truly he was "the servant of sinners, for Christ's sake." He knew the value of a soul, whether it belonged to a prince or the meanest of the human race.

After Mr. Crabb had thus spoken, Mary Carter, a venerable gipsy, was introduced on the platform, on her earnest request to be allowed to say a few words. She said, with great fervency—

" Kind Christian friends,—I bless the day that I was born a gipsy, but I more bless the day that I met Mr. Crabb, now by my side. I bless God, kind people, that I was reclaimed from a wandering life, and brought to a knowledge of the Lord, after spending many of my best years in the service of the wicked one. I thank these kind gentlemen for what they are about to do, and I wish and pray that many of our tribe now standing about here may be brought to that knowledge which blesses the declining days of poor old Mary Carter. Many of you now present, perhaps, despise us—I know some of you do —but I hope you will not continue to do it, for there never was a people more belied than the gipsies. But look above, for God found us out. Thank God and all good friends for this : I hope that many of the poor, orphan, destitute, and other gipsy children will, through the means of this school, commenced for bringing the despised gipsy tribe within the pale, be brought to a knowledge of Christ, and made useful and industrious men and women, walking in the fear of the Lord. May the Lord bless you all ! "

This gipsy woman is still living, and resides with her sister (whose prayer was read by Mr. Crabb) in South-ampton. They are both witnesses for Christ, and longing to depart and be with Him. Each time I have been privileged to have communion with them, I have felt that the Lord still lengthens out their days, that men may see what His grace can do, *even for a gipsy*.

The annual meetings were continued by Mr. Crabb down to the year 1847, when, in consequence of the failure of his health and the infirmities of age, he could no longer continue them ; and from this time the work was transferred from the Southampton Committee to the gentlemen who had the management of the Farnham Institution. The last anniversary (being the 19th) was held in the grounds attached to the mansion of William Betts, Esq., of Bevois Mount, in Southampton, in the month of December, 1848 ; on which occasion Mr. Crabb sent an address to the gipsies from his sick room, in which, as a dying man who loved their souls, and was concerned for their salvation, he besought them to flee from the wrath to come, and exhorted them to place their children where they might be instructed both for time and for eternity. The annual meetings were after this discontinued. They were attended with considerable expense and trouble ;

and no one who had not Mr. Crabb's ardent love for souls would have submitted to the labour and inconvenience which they occasioned.

It is proper to record, that during the eighteen anniversary meetings held by Mr. Crabb, the gipsies conducted themselves in a most becoming and grateful manner, and were never known to commit an act of depredation upon his premises. At one of the meetings, Mr. Sturges Bourne, stated that in his experience as a magistrate for a long series of years, he had never known a quarter session or assizes held in the county in which there was not a gipsy amongst the prisoners: but that since the labours of Mr. Crabb, and his associates for the amelioration of that race of people, there had not been one of them for trial. It may be added, that the name of Mr. Crabb was known and reverenced, as it still is, amongst that people throughout the kingdom. Many of them stood quite in awe of him; and I have known cases of gipsy women, who, when they have solicited persons to have their fortunes told, having been asked if they knew Mr. Crabb, have been ashamed, and walked away; for in their conscience they knew they were doing wrong, and were afraid of losing their characters with him.

It is grievous to say that the Farnham Institution, not having been supported as it deserved, has not been productive of the results which were expected. Forty-six children only have been admitted into it since its erection, being a period of six years; and from various causes the number now within its walls does not exceed five. Those who have left the Institution were instructed in sound religious principles; and in addition to the ordinary rudiments of education, the boys were instructed in spade-husbandry, and the girls in knitting, &c. Some of them obtained situations; but the greater part, from the want of means, or for other reasons, returned to their parents.

The discontinuance of the annual meetings lessened, as might have been expected, the interest which, in Mr. Crabb's time, was felt in behalf of the gipsies; and as the difficulty of obtaining access to them became greatly increased, the Committee of the Farnham Asylum began to, and still, employ a missionary, acquainted with their habits, to visit their camps at Norwood, Barnes, Putney, Bow, Wandsworth, and other places ; and judging from the report of the Committee for the year 1852, he appears to be doing the work of an Evangelist among them with some success. But there has evidently been a retrogression since Mr. Crabb's days, and it may be questioned whether the interest which his labours excited will not die away altogether.

And to what, it may be asked, is this to be traced ? Is it that the hand of God is against the endeavours made to reclaim these wanderers of our land ? Is His mercy "clean gone" from them for ever? Has He proclaimed against them the awful doom, " Let them alone ? " Ye Christian men and women, who compass sea and land to make known the Gospel to the savage Kaffir and the debased Hottentot,—who lift up your voices against the cruelties of Juggernaut, —the infantile and parricidal sacrifices of the Ganges,—who weep as you read of the sorrows of those who,—in that land where men belie their principles, and set at naught the Divine injunction, " Thou shalt love thy neighbour as thyself,"—are made slaves and bondsmen because they differ in colour, and are too feeble to resist injustice, — will you avert your eyes from these outcasts of your native land? Will you leave them to perish around your homesteads and your parks without one effort for their temporal or eternal good? Oh! better were it for them if our legislators enacted their banishment to the inhospitable regions of Greenland, or the burning sands of Africa, for there would the self-denying missionary find them out; there might they hear of Him who came to seek and to save the lost; there, even there, they might feel your sympathy, and be made partakers of your bounty!

Ye sons and daughters of mysterious race,—ye living monuments of England's shame, depart every one of you to some distant island of the further seas, and there make known your desolation and your wants. Let the rude winds waft your cries for help to British ears, quick to catch the distant sound of woe, but deaf to that which is near; tell English Christians that you are no better instructed than heathens; that your souls perish for lack of knowledge. No matter if you have murdered their missionaries, or stirred up rebellion against their honoured and peaceful sovereign, you shall soon behold some mission ship, with its Bethel flag streaming in the wind, glide into your harbours with the gospel of salvation. Your children shall be clothed with habiliments worked by the hand of Albion's fairest daughters; you and your offspring shall no longer lodge through the cold damp night under the canopy of heaven, or eat the bread which you cannot honestly obtain; but you and they shall be brought to lisp a precious Saviour's name, and Christian love shall lavish upon you all her blandishments and care. But remain at home, and you shall nurture your children in sin, teach them the vocabulary of crime, practise them in the arts of iniquity, and you and they shall pass away unheeded, unknown, and unpitied to an eternity of woe, there to curse for ever the country that gave you nothing but a grave.

CHAPTER XIII.

Mr. Crabb's labours amongst the excavators employed on the Southampton Docks.—Preaches to them.—His tract, entitled " Eli Samson."—Two last entries in his Diary.—Reflections on over-engagement in the business of religion.—Irvingism and Tractarianism in Southampton.

IT might well be imagined that, with so much to occupy his time and tax the energies of his mind, Mr. Crabb would rather have circumscribed than enlarged the sphere of his operations; but believing that it should be unto him according to his faith, he could not bear to lose an opportunity of doing, or attempting to do, good to his fellow-men. Accordingly, we find him, in the year 1840, engaged in another work, which required no little labour and self-denial. An Act of Parliament having been obtained for the formation of the present Docks at Southampton, 1,500 excavators and workmen were set to work upon them. These men, with their wives and children, formed a great addition to the population of Southampton; and as most of them were of dissolute habits, Mr. Crabb dreaded the demoralization likely to ensue from their location in the town. Upon their arrival in Southampton, he began his operations by visiting them at their place of work, and distributing amongst such of them as could read, suitable tracts ; and as soon as they were settled in habitations, he visited their families, and affectionately exhorted them to attend the services of the Sabbath in the churches and chapels of the town, and to send their children to be instructed in the parochial and Sabbath-schools. In a short time he established two or three weekly services, which he conducted within a large tent, which was set up in the marsh adjoining the works, and which were attended by many of the men and their families ; and as many of them could neither read nor write, he opened an evening-school in the Seamen's Chapel for their gratuitous instruction, of which many availed themselves.

The moral and spiritual condition of these men was so deplorable, that Mr. Crabb lost no opportunity of bringing before them the evils of sin, and proclaiming the gospel of Christ. One of them—a young man, who had received no education, and was wholly ignorant of God and His truth—having been attacked with a mortal disease, was in his last illness brought to repentance, and gave unquestionable evidence before his death of conversion to God. This event was too important to be lost sight of by Mr. Crabb, who immediately drew up and published a tract, entitled, "A Short Account of the Last Days of Eli Samson; addressed to the Navigators employed on the Works of the Southampton Docks;" 4,000 copies of which were in a few days distributed in Southampton. This tract, which is written in an affectionate strain, contains much Christian truth, enforced in a striking way, and is full of affecting anecdotes and awakening appeals to the conscience ; and there is every reason to believe that it was made extensively useful to the excavators, many of whom, after its publication, became much changed in their conduct, and began to attend the house of God on the Sabbath. The republication of this tract, with a view to its circulation amongst the workmen employed on the railroads and other public works, might be attended with much good.

The tent-services established by Mr. Crabb were continued by him until a clergyman of the Established Church was appointed to act as chaplain to the navigators and their families, when he considered it proper to discontinue his services; but he continued—with the entire concurrence of the chaplain, who was no bigot, and whose path he had cleared from many difficulties, and who was fully sensible of the value of his assistance—to visit them and their families at their houses, and otherwise to labour for their spiritual benefit.

Although Mr. Crabb was thus actively engaged in the laborious undertakings which have been already noticed, he was not oblivious of the duty which he owed to those over whom the Lord had made him overseer. As early as the year 1828, he had two schoolmasters acting under him, one of whom instructed the children at Kingsland, and the other the children of the schools attached to his chapel; and these two labourers were eminently useful, not only during his absence from Southampton, but whilst he was there, in visiting the sick; and both of them having talents for preaching, officiated during his absence, at the Bethel and elsewhere.

From the year 1828 down to the time when his labours ceased, he was too much occupied in the Lord's vineyard to be able to keep up his Diary; so that he has left no record of his labours or Christian experience during that period. The two last entries in his Diary are dated the 14th of July, 1826, and the 5th of July, 1828; and as

they show the state of his mind, and refer to the conflicts
which at those busy periods of his life he had to endure, I
give them at length :

" 14th July, 1826.—Many and great are the conflicts which
I have daily. My mind is discouraged under a deep and abiding sense of my unfaithfulness to my adorable Redeemer, and
not a little at my unfitness for ministerial duties ; but I fear
after thirty years' employment in that blessed work, I am looking too much at my infirmities and not enough to Christ. I
truly lament that I have not read my Bible more. Did I
preach more in Scripture language, I think I should be more
useful, for it is the word of God which is the sword of the
Spirit, and God has promised to bless it. I have for some
time been afflicted with symptoms of asthma, from which I
suffered in a great degree thirty-two years ago, but I feel all is
well. If death be at hand, heaven will follow. I am enabled
to cast my soul on the redeeming blood of Christ ; and for
ever blessed be His name, He condescends to love me, and will
bring me to glory. I am desirous of living until I have placed
on trust, and paid for, my chapel. I am truly in earnest about
it, and hope—yes, believe, my blessed heavenly Father will
meet my wishes and hear my prayers. I regret that I have
not more time for prayer, reading, and study ; for as I am so
fatigued by walking through the day, I want more rest on my ,
bed than I did when I was young. Ah ! youth is the time for
labour. Until eleven o'clock my doors are open to all the poor,
and to those who want advice in trouble, in embarrassed circumstances, family troubles, or soul trouble, of which I have a
great number daily. Then I have my builders and infant-
schools, then my flock and the sick are visited. My letters
take up much of my time. Oh, my blessed and adorable
Redeemer, give me thy strength and consolations, and then I
need not fear. I rejoice to see what God is doing amongst
the great and honourable of the land. Many of them are
coming in from the east and from the west, the north and
the south, not only in Britain, but in various parts of the
world. Glory be to God that I am a living witness of this ! "

5th February, 1828.—Eighteen months have elapsed since

I made a memorandum of the goodness of God to me. I regret this, as so many important events have passed by unrecorded; but I have seldom five minutes in which I am not fully engaged. Precious, precious time! My chapel and school-house are settled on trust fourteen months since, and I have engaged to collect £2,300 for the new Female Penitentiary. It is an arduous work in which I have been engaged twelve months already, and I have collected nearly half of it. It retards for the present my own plans relating to the debt on my chapel and school-house very much, and exposes me to great difficulties, but I could not resist offering my services, as it would not otherwise have been built. O! my God, give me perseverance in the great work. I have yet £2,600 to collect for my chapel-school and Penitentiary, and feel my body and spirits much weaker than a few years since. Nothing less than God's power can enable me to persevere   Oh, my God, be near to me! I am awfully tempted and harassed by Satan to despond; yea, to complain of God. His arrows are very sharp and numerous; but the shield of faith repels them My God will help me. When I am not at home, my two schoolmasters, who preach, now take my duties on the week-day evenings (which is nearly every night), and visit the sick for me, but, oh! I want to be at my pastoral duty. 'T is my great cross to be deprived of that delight; but the cross is the way to heaven, and in my present employment I feel assured I am labouring for generations yet unborn. I am not now gathering knowledge from books, and delighting my soul with their sweets, but if I can be the instrument of giving the bread of life to starving souls, oh, that I may be thankful!"

That excessive occupation in the business of religion —even like that in which Mr. Crabb was at this time so deeply engaged—is a hindrance to personal piety, by abridging closet duties, exhausting the spiritual energies, diverting the mind from the inner circle of the Christian's self, and fixing it on those things which are without, is, notwithstanding the unwillingness of most men to acknowledge it, unquestionable. "Leave me alone, or I shall preach myself into hell!" was the solemn saying of a minister who, when he came to London, was so importuned by his friends to preach day after day, as to have no time to devote to his own soul; and in a sense, he was right, for nothing can be a substitute for closet duties, by which alone the wheels of spiritual life are kept in motion; and where there is no time for self-examination, the growing corruptions of the heart are left undetected, and the true gauge of the spiritual state unascertained. Mr. Crabb was no stranger to these truths, and this led him to strive to make every business in which he was engaged an ordinance in which he could not only serve the Lord, but have communion with Him.

It was an invariable rule with Mr. Crabb never to interfere with politics, or things which did not come within the province of a minister of Christ; but he was always ready to contend for the faith once delivered to the saints, and combat against heresy from whatever quarter it emanated. No sooner, therefore, were the doctrines of Irvingism openly promulgated in the town of Southampton, than he took up his pen and lifted up his voice against them. Amongst other tracts which he published against this heresy, was one entitled "An Address on Irvingism," in which he so plainly exposed the errors of that delusive system, that many were delivered from its snares, and others saved from falling into them.

The Tractarian heresy soon afterwards began to infect Southampton, when he again unfurled the standard of truth, for he felt that this heresy was more to be dreaded than Irvingism, inasmuch as it was "brought in" by ministers of a true church, and was so mingled with truth, that the unwary and uninstructed were easily seduced and carried away by it. The baneful influence of this anti-Protestant system was soon felt in the town. In the course of a short time, two of the Church ministers began to preach against Evangelical truth, setting up baptism in the place of regeneration by the Spirit, lifting up the sacrament of the Lord's supper instead of the Lord himself, and substituting forms and ceremonies in the place of spiritual worship and spiritual life.

One of these ministers having issued a brief pastoral letter to his parishioners, in which he exhorted them to bring their children to be baptized as the only way to make them Christians, and invited them to the Lord's supper as a means of grace without reference to their faith or practice, Mr. Crabb published a letter in reply, in which he exposed the unscriptural character of these views and the injurious effects which such a system of Christianity made easy was calculated to produce; and from this time he scarcely ever preached without exposing the growing heresies of the day, and exhorting his hearers to study the word of God as the only antidote to doctrines so palpably opposed to the teaching of the Lord Jesus and his Apostles.

CHAPTER XIV.

Mr. Crabb's Tracts: "Mary Ann Kean"—"William Cawte "—
"Herbert Bamfield"—"A Warning Voice to Drunkards and
Pugilists "—" The Races."—His other publications.—Anecdote.
—His seventieth year commemorated at the Long Rooms.—
The address made to him.—His speech.

THE Book of God's providential dealings with the
Church and the world was much studied by Mr. Crabb ;
and he never allowed any solemn or striking providence,
either public or private, where it could be made spiritually
useful, to go unimproved. Thus most of the tracts which
he published have relation to events, which, at the time
when they were written, engaged the attention of the
public or some particular class of the community.

One of them, entitled " Salvation by Christ, experienced in the Last Months of Mary Ann Keen, a Naviga-
tor's Wife," was written for the spiritual benefit of the
navigators then at work upon the new docks at Southampton, and its design was to show the evils consequent upon
the imprudent marriage of young women with men whose
moral character they have not ascertained—to depict the
awful consequence of sin, especially drunkenness, and to
set forth the readiness of God to receive even the prodigal
who comes back only to die.

Another tract, "The Grace of God Magnified in the
Conversion and Happy Death of William Cawte," consists
of a narrative of the last days of a young man in whose

heart a deep work of grace had been wrought, and its object was to show the realities of that work in the peace it brings to the individual himself, the deep concern it begets in him for the salvation of others, and the glory which redounds to God from the sinner's salvation.

Another; "The Truth of the Christian Religion exemplified in the Early Religious Impressions, and the Christian Experience, and Happy Death of Vernon Herbert Bamfield, who died in his Fifteenth Year," was designed to impress upon the young the importance of remembering their Creator in the days of their youth, and to encourage Christian parents in the arduous duties connected with the training of their children.

Another of his tracts was entitled, "A Warning Voice to Drunkards and Pugilists," to which was appended an address "to Publicans and Masters of Gin-shops;" and originated in the circumstance of a profligate and abandoned woman having been burnt to death in a state of intoxication, whilst all the persons who lived in the house with her had gone to witness a pugilistic encounter on Shirley Common. In this tract, of which 10,000 were published for the first Edition, the seller of intoxicating liquors is thus solemnly addressed:

"Who pays the four millions of taxation annually on spirits? Chiefly the poor drunkard: and every night, he that sells most of the fatal poison, may reflect thus,— I have added more than any of my fellow-creatures to the increase of real misery in the world; I have driven the poor to the overseer for relief; I have helped to fill the poorhouses with the starving and dying; I have filled the pawnshops with the garments of the poor, and the mechanic's only means of life, his tools for labour; I have sent home the poor man penniless, in a drunken state, to

I

his starving wife and children, who has sometimes beaten
her almost to death; I have been the means of many a
sad broil, which perhaps has ended in death; I have
assisted in filling the prisons, hulks, and also in peopling
the Colonies, to which so many hundreds of wretched
beings are transported every year. I am increasing the
bankrupt's list, crowding the prisons with debtors, and
swelling the calendar of prisoners with *my friends* who
supported me in my plans, and helped me to amass so
much wealth; I am adding to the number of unhappy
women who throng our streets by night; yes, I live on
their filthy, cursed, soul-destroying wages every night;
my poisonous draughts also encourage servants to rob
their masters to supply their artificial and supposed wants;
I have helped to ruin in my house hundreds of tradesmen;
I am filling the lunatic asylums with wretched patients; I
am the means of causing hundreds of bad men and women
to break God's fourth commandment, which is *Remember
that thou keep holy the Sabbath day.* The fact is, I
have had their hats, their shoes, their coats, their gowns,
their linen, and almost all they poᵴ ess, that they may
drink of my ' *drops of life,*' my ' *cordial gin.*' But,
ah! what is this to the scenes that ᵗ ¹ be exposed to
public view at the bar of Christ?—for God has said, in His
book, that ' *no drunkard shall inherit the kingdom of
heaven.*' Then look forward to the Judgment, when with
all those drunkards who have died, or may die *in their
sins*, there must be a meeting at the bar of God. You must
meet there; for '*We must all appear before the Judg-
ment-seat of Christ; that* EVERY ONE *may receive the
things done in his body, according to that he hath done,
whether it be good or bad.*' What a meeting!! O! who
can bear the thought of it?"

One of the most fruitful sources of drunkenness and debauchery in Southampton, was that worst of all abominations in a Christian land, that never-failing magnet which attracts to it all the villany, vice, and profligacy of the surrounding country—*the Race-course*. The effects which it produced on the morals of the lower orders of Southampton were known by those only who searched them out and saw them as Mr. Crabb did. Year after year he preached against this fruitful source of vice, and in his visitations throughout the town warned the people against it. Soon after he settled in Southampton, he published a tract, entitled "The Races," in which he pourtrayed the evils resulting from them to individuals and to society at large. Six thousand copies of this tract were distributed throughout Southampton, at the expense of Lady ——; it passed through many editions, and Mr. Crabb had the satisfaction to know that it was made extensively useful.

Besides the tracts already referred to, Mr. Crabb was the author of the following publications :

"The Life of Captain Bazin."

"The Gipsies' Advocate."

" A Brief Account of the Gipsies of England. "

"The Mournful Remembrancer; being an Account of a Dreadful Fire in Southampton, in which Twenty-one Lives were lost."

Two series of Tracts against Popular Infidelity, entitled "Consider the End :" &c., &c.

There is no pretence to authorship in these books and tracts. They were written for the benefit of the humbler classes, and are addressed to them in a style adapted to their capacities. They are full of incident, and abound with Scripture truth set forth in a way calculated to

attract and touch the heart.   Having been written for the
glory of God, and distributed in faith, doubtless they
were not written nor distributed in vain, for the mouth of
the Lord has spoken it, "My word shall not return to me
void."

The sums of money received from the sale of these
tracts, and which in the aggregate were of no small
amount, were applied by Mr. Crabb in that cause for
which alone he desired to live—the advancement of the
Redeemer's glory upon earth.

There is a circumstance connected with the sale of the
tract, entitled "Jane Thring," that deserves to be noticed.
So great was the interest which it created, that Mr. Crabb
was importuned by the hawkers to let them have copies
for sale throughout the country.   One of these men
obtained a large number of copies from Mr. Crabb, for
sale in the Isle of Wight, upon the representation that he
had been an Infidel, and having embraced the truth,
desired to make it known.   This man, however, turned
out to be a depraved hypocrite, and he and a woman who
travelled with him sold the tracts, and never accounted
with Mr. Crabb for the proceeds.   It happened, however,
in the providence of God, that as they journeyed through
the island, a farmer engaged in ploughing was induced by
the solicitation of the woman to purchase one of the tracts
at half price, and it pleased God by his Spirit to bring
home to his heart the Gospel truth which it so plainly
and powerfully set forth, and to make it the means of his
conversion.   Having been brought into much soul-trouble,
he went to Southampton to seek an interview with Mr.
Crabb, and, being a timid man, in order to avoid any
questions at home as to the object of his visit, he chose a
market day, when it might be supposed he went upon

business. Such, however, was his timidity, that after several ineffectual attempts to call at Mr. Crabb's dwelling, he returned home without seeing him. The circumstance was made known to Mr. Crabb, who, some time afterwards, having an engagement to preach in the Isle of Wight, called upon the farmer, and, to his great joy, heard from his lips an account of his conversion. Like Barnabas at Antioch, Mr. Crabb, having seen the grace of God, was glad, and exhorted the farmer, that "with purpose of heart he would cleave unto the Lord." This he appears to have done, and he never forgot what he owed to Mr. Crabb's tract; and after a lapse of fourteen years he wrote to him, telling him that as he supposed he was then becoming infirm and less able to walk, he was about to send him a pony for his use. The pony was soon on the road, but having fallen down and injured one of his knees, the farmer not liking to send it to Mr. Crabb in that state, took it home again. Having, however, shortly afterwards disposed of it for £7, he forwarded the money to Mr. Crabb, with a statement of the circumstances under which he sent it.

"Now," observes Mr. Crabb in his Diary, " mark the providence of God : £7 was what I lost by the man who took my tracts, and here is a man blessed in reading one and he sends me the exact sum I lost. 'Whoso is wise and will observe these things, shall understand the loving-kindness of the Lord.'"

Having noticed the principal events in Mr. Crabb's life in succession, without regard to chronological arrangement, which would have rendered the narration of them indistinct, we are now brought to follow him through his declining years, when

" By unperceived degrees he wore away."

Upon looking back at his early career, the state of his health during that period, and the incessant toils he endured throughout his life, we may be well surprised to find him at the age of seventy still strong in body, active in mind, and diligent in service;—but so it was. He still preached and laboured—still carried on the warfare in which for so many years he had been engaged against Satan and the world, and still contemplated new methods of advancing the glory of the Master he had so long loved and served, and adding fresh conquests to his kingdom on earth. Upon attaining the age of seventy, his congregation and friends being anxious to testify their respect for his disinterested and useful labours during the last twenty years in Southampton, determined on a public tea-meeting to commemorate his birthday, and accordingly, on the 16th of April, 1844, the Long-rooms were fitted up for the occasion, and, under the direction of the officers of the Peninsular and Oriental steamers, their men decorated the rooms with a profusion of flags and evergreens, in the style in which the highest commander in the navy of England would be honoured. Such was the anxiety of persons of all ranks to be present, that early in the afternoon the possessors of tickets began to pour into the lobby to secure admission; and at five o'clock, the time when the majority of the company might have been expected, not a seat was to be obtained by hundreds who crowded wherever they could stand.

Soon after five o'clock Mr. Crabb led into the rooms the lady of the Rev. J. Reynolds, of Rumsey, followed by Mrs. Crabb, his son Mr. James Crabb, and Mr. Reynolds. The Peninsular Steam Company's sailors saluted his entrance from a small battery they had placed in the front of the building, and the firing of each gun was answered by simultaneous applause from one end of the room to the other.

The orchestra was occupied by many of the best vocal and instrumental performers from the different choirs in the town, who, as a voluntary tribute of respect to Mr. Crabb, executed several anthems during the time tea was on the tables.

At seven o'clock the Rev. J. Reynolds took the chair, and after an appropriate hymn had been sung, and a solemn prayer offered to Almighty God for his blessing on the meeting, the assembly was addressed by the Chairman, who, in a kind and appropriate manner, bore the highest testimony to the unsullied integrity of Mr. Crabb through a long life.* Amongst other things, he said that

* The following letter from the Rev. Thomas Adkins, an eminent Congregational minister of Southampton, was read at the meeting, and from the catholic and truly Christian spirit which pervades it, is worthy of being preserved :

" Northampton, April 13, 1844.

" My Beloved Brother,—I address you as the chairman of the interesting meeting that will be held to-morrow evening, in order to evince the regard which his numerous friends cherish towards our revered and estimable brother, Mr. Crabb. I much regret, on several accounts, that I am prevented from being present on that occasion, in order to add my testimony to that of others as to the high estimation in which he is held. I would not 'give the creature his Creator's due ; ' but would rather adopt the language of Job, and say, ' I know not how to give flattering titles, for in so doing my Maker would soon take me away ;' but still we are commanded to give ' honour to whom honour is due,' and therefore I would add, that, as long as eminent piety, catholicity of spirit, active benevolence, unwearied efforts to benefit the souls of men, are causes for profound regard from one man to another, the name of James Crabb will be held in everlasting remembrance, especially in that town in which he has laboured for more than twenty-five years they had known each other. He would with all humility acknowledge that Mr. Crabb was right, and he was wrong, when he tried to dissuade him from coming to settle in Southampton. For three or four years previous to that, they had been in the habit of the closest brotherly intimacy; and his brother Yarnold, whom he was glad to see present, could testify that they were three such years of ministerial friendship and intimacy as three ministers of different denominations were seldom permitted to enjoy. Mr. Crabb saw that Southampton presented to him an extended sphere of usefulness, and he came there; and, through his ministry, many, amongst all sorts and conditions, and in all gradations of society, had been brought under the power of the glorious Gospel of the blessed God.

After referring to the building of Zion Chapel and its opening, he added that Mr. Crabb assumed no denominational character, and to this day he believed that no one could say to what denomination he belonged. (Cheers.) He rejoiced to hear that response. He was well assured their united prayer would be, that their pastor might long be continued amongst them; but when he was gone to his reward, Zion Chapel would be the property of the public; and the trustees, with the church, as they ought to do, would have to exercise the right and respon-

so successfully and so long. I beg you to assure him of my sincere and high regard, my prayers for the continuance of his life and labours, and the Divine blessing on both; and I beg you to communicate, as Chairman, as an act of justice to him and myself, the contents of this hastily written letter to the assembled friends.　　　　" I am, my dear Brother,

" Ever affectionately yours,

" The Rev. John Reynolds.　　　　" THOMAS ADKINS."

sibility of Christians, in choosing their own religious teacher. He rejoiced in this great freedom, and prayed them to stand fast in the liberty wherewith Christ had made them free. To have lived to be threescore and ten, unblemished in character, beloved, esteemed, and revered by multitudes of men of all conditions and of all opinions, was no small honour for a Christian minister. That honour was Mr. Crabb's, and they rejoiced over him and with him, that he was thus honoured and blessed of God. He rejoiced with them at this opportunity of testifying their respect and esteem for their beloved pastor, and of presenting to the throne of heavenly grace their united and hearty supplications that he might long continue to be the honoured instrument of the conversion of multitudes more of immortal beings, and that at last he might finish his course with joy."

The following address to Mr. Crabb, drawn up for the occasion by the Committee, which was received with deep interest, was then read :

" ESTEEMED AND BELOVED PASTOR,

" It is with heartfelt gratitude to Almighty God, that we are permitted, in the course of His providence, to commemorate, at your advanced age, your birth into this fallen world. Your parents are long since laid in the dust; and you are now an old man; you are seventy years of age. Few of our common family,—which a sublime Jewish prophet, and an inspired Christian apostle, pronounce to be but grass, because generation after generation we are mown down by the scythe of death,—reach the age in which we see you in comparative health and strength—the age of 'three score years and ten'— the period declared by the pen of inspiration, three thousand years since, as the full age of mortal man.

"We have been too well instructed by your pulpit ministrations, to offer to you any other congratulations than those which we think your God and ours, through the merits of our only Saviour, Jesus Christ, will graciously look upon with complacency. We, therefore, only approach you, on this interesting occasion, to congratulate you on the wonderful mercy of our heavenly Father to you, his kind and faithful ambassador, in so graciously sparing your life, and making your labours among us so continuously successful. For many are both the dead and the livᵗ to whom the instructions of your lips have been insᵗ⋅⋅ ᵗ tal of their conversion to God.

.. ᵤ think it not inappropriate, as a part of our present celebration, to review for a moment or two the more prominent instances of your ministerial usefulness ; not, as we have already intimated, to offend you with any adulation, but as expressive of our sincere thankfulness to our heavenly Father, for His abundant grace bestowed upon you and us, in Christ Jesus our Lord.

"We do not forget that, at a very early period of your ministerial labours, it pleased God to make you instrumental of that very remarkable conversion, narrated by the pious clergyman, Legh Richmond, under the designation of 'The Dairyman's Daughter.'* Nor are we forgetful of your known and acknowledged usefulness for a period of thirty years after that interesting event.

"But it is your settling in Southampton, when you were approaching your fiftieth year—when you had acquired extensive knowledge of the world, and of the church —and when your attachment to Christianity, and your

* A narrative of her conversion will be found in page 192.

sympathy for sinners, were matured—that we look back upon as the period when you were to be more eminently useful as a faithful preacher of the Gospel. The highway, the green field, the open place, the ship's deck, and the rooms we now so happily occupy, were the first theatres of your more enlarged labours. And happy are we that they were but 'like the drops before the shower;' that they were, in reality, the beginning of extensive ministerial usefulness.

"We have seen successively rise up, under your personal care, useful and prosperous institutions. As the first of those institutions we may mention the building Zion Chapel, and the formation of our present church. When we consider that that chapel is paid for, through 'r own unwearied exertions, and that our church has .... on gradually increasing for a number of years, under your exclusive pastoral care; we cannot but consider you as highly favoured by the providence and grace of God. That your difficulties were numerous, that your anxieties have been many, and that your labours have been very great, must be apparent to every one in the least acquainted with the troubles which usually attend such undertakings. But through all these troubles, we are most thankful to say, has God safely brought you. And we can now thankfully sit in our seats in the house of our God, and listen to the expositions you are still enabled to give us, without the fear that pecuniary difficulties will ever damp the energies of your declining life and labours, or ever take off our attention from the words of your mouth.

"We cannot but regard your labours, we may say, your very successful labours, among the outcasts of society, with very pleasing and grateful emotions; for not only were your instructions and prayers blessed to the most

happy conversion of Jane Thring, but your narrative of
that conversion, under the title of 'The Penitent Magdalene,' has resulted in the erection of institutions which do
honour to our country.   And we are happy that your care
is still actively extended to the first of those institutions,
the Penitentiary of this town and county.

"It would be wrong for us to overlook the very active
part you have taken in the education of the rising generation.   Not only were you the first who introduced the
education of infants into Southampton, but you have excited your friends, the members of your church and congregation, to engage extensively in Sabbath-school instruction.   And we rejoice, that four day-schools and four
Sunday-schools, at which several hundreds of children are
regularly, and, we hope we may say, efficiently instructed
in the truths of the inspired word of our God, are in
operative existence.

"If we cannot congratulate you on an equal success
attending your unwearied labours among our seamen ; we
rejoice that your care for their instruction does not de-
crease, and that your exertions have not been in vain.   We
are assured that your weekly and monthly services on
board the Peninsular and Oriental steamers, as well as
your occasional expositions on board the *Atalanta,* and
your Monday evening discourses in your Bethel of this
port, are collectively attended by a great mass of sailors,
whose behaviour during Divine service is very serious and
devout.   And no doubt but that the seed of Divine truth
sown in the hearts of the frank 'sons of ocean,' will one
day take root, and bear an abundant harvest to the glory
of the grace of God.

"We cannot omit to mention your long continued atten-
tions and instructions to a race of men whose wandering

habits have almost seemed to preclude the expectation of genuine and established piety among them. But your patience has been great, and God has mercifully rewarded it, even in the thorough reformation of many gipsies, some of whom are with us to-day, whose hearts, no doubt, have already anticipated us in this part of our congratulatory address.

"But we do not hide from ourselves, and we do not wish to hide from you, the perpetual labours in which you have abounded towards the sick and poor in their own houses. Permit us to remind you, that several very remarkable conversions have resulted from your visits of this kind. And for this we would catch the joy of the angels of heaven, and say, 'The name of the Lord be praised.' We would not be unmindful of the charity of your Sunday evening's congregation, which has for twenty years enabled you to afford a weekly gratuity to the more necessitous of your sick sufferers.

"Permit us, in conclusion, beloved Pastor, to say, that not only do we rejoice in the cordial union you evidently feel towards Christians of all denominations, and in the present prosperous state of your church; but more particularly do we rejoice in the increasing faithfulness and usefulness of your ministry. Your late lectures against infidelity, and your many late cautions against popular delusions and heresies, we hope will not be in vain. We hope they will be made a blessing to the crowded assemblies which have heard them with so much apparent interest. We are convinced that it is your sincere desire to preach unto us the whole Gospel of our Lord Jesus Christ. And we pray that you may be long spared to preside over us in the Lord, and that we shall also have grace imparted to us from above, to continue an affectionate and united people, walking in the counsel of the Lord our God."

Mr. Crabb, more humbled than elevated by these respectful and fervid commendations, replied to the address as follows:

" My dear Friends,

" I have never been under such an ordeal in all my life as this evening, and never wish to be again, unless it were for your good. Indeed I have been very deeply affected with all the bustle that such a poor old sinner as I am have this day made. I hope, however, I feel grateful for the testimony borne in my favour, by my honest, faithful, and beloved brother Reynolds, whom I have so well and so long known, and loved so much. And, I assure you, my friends, I am much affected with the warm address of my church and people. I do not know how they have got together all the facts to which they have referred, but I cannot but admit they have told a pretty correct tale. And though I am not fond of fine things being said about me, I receive their address at this time as a sincere testimony of their affection for me as their pastor. I respect that part of the address which refers to the good blessing of God upon my labours : indeed, it does appear to me that God has greatly blessed me, or how could I have succeeded in the way I have? When I began to build Zion Chapel, I had but a hundred pounds subscribed towards that great undertaking, and yet I have never been embarrassed for money. Some of my friends have said it was built in faith : so it was. I believed that God would be with me, and he really was with me ; for I received help in a manner truly astonishing to myself. One sent me five pounds; another ten ; another twenty; another fifty; and, when my

congregation got so crowded, one gentleman gave me
money for an end gallery; and, soon after, that gentleman
and others added two side galleries. And now, chapel and
galleries are all paid for. This support was the more remarkable, as many of the larger contributors to my plans
knew comparatively little of me: and the greater number
of them I had never seen. Indeed I believe, as I believe
I live, that my coming to Southampton was entirely under
the direction of the providence of God.

" But there is one thing in the address of my affectionate
Church which is not named. I allude to the circumstances
which more particularly determined me to come to this
town. The intention, indeed, had long been on my mind.
I usually, after the school hours in the evening, came to
Southampton to visit on a sick bed the daughter of a mer-
chant. And it was more particularly in my solitary walks
to Rumsey, often at a late hour, that I turned the subject
of coming here over in my mind. I saw the increasing
destitution of the town. Indeed, I saw the increase of
everything but places in which the people might worship
God. Professional men of every description had increased.
Merchants, and tradesmen, and public-houses had increased; but there was no increase of churches and chapels.
So great a burden was this upon my heart, that I was
drawn out in daily and earnest prayer that God would open
my way. On one of these occasions my beloved wife said
to me, ' Why, James, what are you praying so about
now?' And as she has ever been a good, sincere, affectionate wife, adviser, and friend to me, I said to her, ' I am
praying that God will direct me in my determination to fix
at Southampton.' For some time she could not see, with
me, that that was my duty; but after a while she said to
me, one morning after prayers, ' Well, I should be very

sorry to throw any obstacle in your way, if you think of going to Southampton : yet I confess I cannot see your way clear; but if you see it right, go in the name of the Lord.' And I did come, and take and open the rooms in which I now speak. But I assure you, my dear friends, I did not come, even then, rashly. As I have said, the religious destitution of the town had long been known, and has long been a cause of deep sorrow to me. At last a melancholy circumstance determined me to open these rooms for Sabbath preaching. A man preached in the small room adjoining this, who preached the gospel, but lived scandalously. By and by his scandalous living was found out, and his congregation was scattered. I was very grieved that the poor people should be scattered, and I determined to re-open these rooms. My view was to come and gather up the poor neglected church-people, so I published a bill to that effect; and when I had my opening service I said to these poor church-people,—If you will come and hear me preach, those of you who have not sittings in your churches, I will read your prayers morning and evening; but as for you that belong to the Independent, Baptist, and Methodist congregations, let me never see your faces here again; for I am not come to rob churches ; but if you know of any poor wretches who spend their Sabbaths in drunkenness and vice, send them to hear 'Parson Crabb.' And certainly many very vile sinners crowded to hear the word of God. I have said I did not come to rob churches, but I and my people robbed the devil very largely, for hundreds of his vilest servants and slaves, who were known to live most scandalously, have been converted. Of these many were Magdalenes. Jane Thring, and several others, are gone to heaven; and several are regularly kneeling with me at the table of the

Lord, whom I am not ashamed to call my sisters in Christ.

" I have said it is marvellous to me how God has helped me. And, if my life should be spared, I hope He will help me to build a large seamen's chapel, and a school-room for seamen's children. I have preached to seamen occasionally more than fifty years; and I have had weekly services for them in Southampton for the last twenty years. On a Monday night I preach in the mariner's Bethel, or chapel, near the quay, through the winter, and during the summer months I generally occupy a ship's deck, or some part of the quay; I also preach on board the Peninsular and Oriental steamers. And I am happy that the conduct of the sailors is always very serious, and I have great hopes that many of them will be converted to God. I have the honour of being called the seamen's chaplain; and I account it a very high honour; indeed, their salvation lies near my heart. My love to them, I believe, will go on increasing with my years. I was afraid the other day that the directors were going to pay me for preaching on board the Peninsular and Oriental steamers, for they sent me some money down. This, at first, was very horrifying to my feelings, for I do not want money for preaching to sailors. But I soon found out that the money came towards paying off the debt on the infants'-school, and then my mind was easy. Indeed, I do not think I shall be embarrassed for want of the money for the seamen's chapel which I intend to build, if God should spare my life. And while talking of my love to you sailors, I cannot but thank you for the trouble you have taken to ornament this room so with flags. One of the officers of the *Lady Mary Wood* took the pains this morning to explain it all to me, and it appears that you have hung the flags just as if you wished to honour a visit paid you by the Lord High Admiral. I sincerely thank you for your respect and affection, and I hope I shall preach many more sermons to you. I always pray for you, captains, officers, and men, and I hope I shall meet you all in heaven.

"Allusion has been made in the address of my church, read by Mr. Lawes, to my love of the gipsies; and I have to tell you, that we are about to build a school for the education of gipsy children. I am sure we shall get the money. I have now the best coadjutor in the gipsy cause I have ever had since the removal from this town of the good Sir Matthew Blakiston, the Rev. J. West, rector of Chettle, Dorsetshire. A gentleman has given an acre and a half of ground to begin with for the erection of the school.

"Before I sit down I wish to thank you all for your affectionate regards towards me. My long-esteemed friend, Mr. Reynolds; my church and people, who have also made me a present of a new gown; the sailors, whose hands have hung up all these flags, and the choir, who have kindly volunteered their services for the evening; I thank you all."

CHAPTER XV.

ALTHOUGH Mr. Crabb had attained his seventieth year, and his natural strength was somewhat abated, his mind was still active and vigorous. Knowing that there was much work to be done in his Master's vineyard, and that the night was coming, when he could no longer work, he put forth his remaining energies, and determined, "whilst it was called to-day," to be "up and doing." In a letter written by him to a Christian friend, dated two months prior to the public meeting which has been already referred to, he thus narrates the manner in which he then filled up his time:

" All the morning at my table, writing to correspondents, or at my tracts, with which I mean by-and-by to deluge this town,—Tracts on Infidelity, Puseyism, &c. My heart aches at the evils tolerated in the church. In the morning I receive the applications of the poor and distressed in body or mind. At twelve I dine ; then go into the town to visit the sick and dying. I take tea with my wife at five o'clock—at six return to town and renew my visits. Every Monday night I preach at the seamen's chapel—on Tuesdays on board one of the Peninsular steamers—on Wednesdays at my own chapel—on Thursdays at the Penitentiary. I never reach home till half-past ten at night, as I have generally the sick to visit after service. My chapel is crowded to excess, and I have additions to my church at every monthly meeting. Should I live till April I shall be seventy. I am seldom kept from duty. I had an attack of fever two months ago, through visiting two bad cases, when not well myself, and in a state of great exhaustion. I laid by but one day (Saturday) and preached with the fever on me the following day, though with great difficulty. I lost all my skin in the week after, but was soon restored."

He went on thus labouring, sometimes more and sometimes less, till the 3rd of September, 1848, on which day he preached two sermons at Shirley, near Southampton, for the benefit of the Wesleyan schools. The heat arising from the crowded state of the chapel greatly exhausted him; and whilst suffering from its effects, he attended a meeting in his chapel on the Wednesday evening following, on which occasion several of his friends, observing his physical and mental exhaustion, wished, upon the conclusion of the meeting, to accompany him home, but he declined their kind offers. A poor woman, however, who was present followed him on his road homeward; but he had not advanced far when he suddenly fell down under a paralytic seizure. His kind follower—the messenger of Heaven—who was close upon his footsteps, ran to his assistance, and had him conveyed home. This attack was, upon the whole, a slight one, and in the course of a week it pleased the Lord to restore to him the use of his limbs and the full possession of his faculties. This attack, however, was felt by him as a warning that his labours were approaching to a termination and that he had reached the borders of the land which he was about to enter. He therefore began to put his house in

order, that he might be ready to depart at his Lord's
bidding.

Whilst Mr. Crabb was thus waiting his dismissal he
was suddenly called to take a last earthly farewell of
her who, for fifty-one years, had been not only a partner
of his joys and sorrows, but his "helper in Christ." In
the latter end of February, 1849, Mrs. Crabb, who had
then attained her seventy-ninth year, was attacked with
a serious illness, and after languishing until the 2nd
of March, entered into rest. Knowing whom she had
believed, she was not only ready, but rejoiced to depart
and be with Christ.

Mrs. Crabb was a woman of exalted piety, and eminent
Christian attainments. From the time of her marriage
until Mr. Crabb was obliged to be absent from home,
or his labours became so great as to break in upon their
private hours of devotion, she and Mr. Crabb were accustomed to rise at five o'clock for Scripture reading and
prayer, and they invariably spent some time together
daily in devotional exercises. After their family increased,
and Mr. Crabb settled in Rumsey as a schoolmaster, Mrs.
Crabb's time was so taken up with her domestic duties,
which were of a very onerous character, that she had
little time to devote to those out-of-door employments
amongst the poor and the sick in which, at an earlier
period of her life, she delighted to engage. Home—the
most momentous sphere of a Christian's labours, and
yet so much neglected or lost sight of by many—was
from that time the peaceful sphere of her labours, in
which she bore witness for Jesus before her household,
both in word and deed. She did not hinder her husband's ministry, and sadden the hearts of the righteous,
as the wives of some men do, by affectation of rank,

worldliness of spirit, or those many inconsistencies which
serve to make it questionable whether their husbands
know how to rule their own houses, or if they do, whether
they do not allow those things there which not only the
word of God condemns, but they themselves condemn in
their people.   Being possessed of much sagacity and
discernment, she was eminently useful to Mr. Crabb in
secular matters, upon which he was likely, from his unsus-
picious and unselfish character, to make mistakes; and he
had grace to defer to her judgment where he had reason
to distrust his own.   The late holy Richard Adams, of
Lymington, who was no mean authority in spiritual
things, always spoke of her in the most exalted terms.
"I often wondered," he said, "at the success which
attended my brother Crabb's labours; but I soon saw the
secret of it; for whilst he was abroad labouring, his wife
was at home praying.   Oh, how blessed is the portion of
that man—'the happiest of his kind'—whose destiny in
this life is linked with one who, like her, is adorned with
the habiliments of grace, and the ornament of a meek and
quiet spirit,—in whose heart is the fulness of God, and
whose lips speak continually the language of heaven!
How sweet is the intercourse of two such souls! and yet
not two, but one,—one in Christ, and in Him bound to
each other by the ties of a love as unchanging as that
wherewith He has loved His church.   The world may
frown, friends may look coldly on that man, but in all
his trials, with a rejoicing heart he turns his feet homewards to her whose presence can dispel every sorrow, and
compensate for every disappointment; whose participa-
tion of his trials diminishes their burden, and whose
enjoyment of his mercies gives them a duplicity of
measure.   And such had been the experience of Mr.

Crabb in the society of her whose eyes had now closed upon this world; and although he was now old and gray headed, and about soon to follow her, he felt deeply his loss. But he was enabled to rejoice whilst he sorrowed, and in tribulation gave thanks that she had gone to be with Him whom her soul loved, and that he should soon be where he could mingle his praises with hers."

In Mr Crabb's present state of health it had become necessary to provide a substitute for his pulpit, so that the small income he had received from his chapel ceased; and as with the Apostle he could say, "Silver and gold have I none" (for he laid out all he could spare in the Lord's cause), a few of his friends (members of the Church of England), constrained by the love of Christ, made up between them an income of £150, which they paid to him during the remainder of his life.

It was not long before Mr. Crabb had a second and more severe attack of paralysis, which not only rendered him unable to engage in any public duty, but incapacitated him from walking. Having slightly recovered from its effects, he was daily wheeled in a chair to visit the poor and the sick, with whom he conversed and prayed, and whose necessities he never failed to relieve. His visits to the Penitentiary were also frequent. He regularly attended the services of the house of God, from which nothing but an utter impossibility of being carried there could keep him; and when he was so weak as to be unable to creep along the aisle, he was carried on a chair sufficiently near to the pulpit to hear the word read and preached, for like David his soul thirsted for that God who had carried him unto hoar hairs. One Sabbath morning, however, and also on the day of the thanksgiving for the removal of the cholera, being assisted into the pulpit, he addressed his people as

a dying man, exhorting sinners to repentance, and the
people of God, that "with full purpose of heart they
would cleave unto the Lord." His last appearance
amongst his people was on Wednesday evening, in the
month of August, 1851. Though suffering from extreme
weakness, he was carried down to his chapel, and from the
reading desk addressed them from John xiii. 7. After
this day he grew weaker and weaker. He had now no
more triumphs to achieve, no more battles to fight; he had
finished his course. He, therefore, took off his helmet,
battered in many a conflict, laid down his shield, pierced
with many a dart, at the feet of Him whom he had so long
served, and could now no longer serve; and like Simeon,
was ready and willing to depart. On the 11th September,
1851, he was again attacked with paralysis, and remained
for thirty-six hours in a state of insensibility. Although
little hope was entertained of his restoration, he, by
degrees, recovered the use of his mental powers and the
faculty of speech, so as to be enabled to converse with his
family, and a few friends who were admitted to see him,
on the blessed change that awaited him, and to speak of
the comfort he enjoyed from the full realisation of those
truths he had so long proclaimed to others. He was in
the full possession of that hope which maketh not ashamed,
and of that peace which is the result of a good conscience.
As a "gallant ship," laden with precious freight, after
having been buffeted by storms, and driven about by
contrary winds, enters with a propitious gale her destined
haven, so he was now, after the toils and afflictions of a
long life, about to have "an abundant entrance ministered
into him into the everlasting kingdom." On inquiring
of a medical friend whether he was near his end, and being
told that he was visibly declining, "Glorious news," said

he; " I desire to go home. Jesus is all in all to me."
His friend said, " You will see Him in His own time."
" Yes," he replied, " He is all wise and all good." He
was observed to be much in prayer, and frequently heard
to repeat the well-known verse,

> " Jesus, thy blood and righteousness
> My beauty are, my glorious dress ;
> Midst flaming worlds in these array'd,
> With joy shall I lift up my head."

On Saturday, the 13th, he was visited by his kind
friend, the Lady Elizabeth O—. Upon her beginning
to quote the text, " Jesus Christ the same—" he took
up, with a heavenly expression, " yesterday, to-day, and
for ever." Looking at his daughter-in-law he said, " All
Christ, nothing in me;" and this, as Lady O— truly
remarked, was the secret of his life.

Such was his desire to witness for his Lord to the last,
even with his dying breath, that on the Monday following,
though suffering from extreme weakness, he had the youths
who were under the tuition of his son James brought to
his bed-side, and spoke to them, as a dying man, upon the
love of that Saviour who had died the just for the unjust,
and bade them see with what joy and peace, trusting in
Him, he could welcome death.

On Tuesday he was weaker, and it was evident that
his " earthly house of this tabernacle" was about to be
dissolved. He remained in a state of calm repose during
the day, and fell asleep in Jesus about half-past four on
Wednesday, the 17th September, 1851.

> " Sure the last end
> Of the good man is peace !—How calm his exit !
> Night dews fall not more gently to the ground,
> Nor weary worn-out winds expire so soft !"

K

So placid was his countenance in death, that it was difficult for those who gazed upon it to realise that it was not him, but his tenement of clay.

> " He smiled in death, and still his cold pale face
> Retain'd that smile. As when a waveless lake,
> In which the wintry stars all bright appear
> Is sheeted by a nightly frost with ice,
> Still it reflects the face of heav'n unchanged,
> Unruffled by the storm or sweeping blast."

It having been the wish of Mr. Crabb that his remains should be carried to their resting-place by some of the sailors of the Peninsular and Oriental Steam Navigation Company, his wish was complied with, and he was interred in the same grave with his wife, in the Southampton Cemetery. Amongst the afflictions which Mr. Crabb was called to endure, was that of losing all his children in their youth, except three sons, who survive him.

Such was the life, of which but a faint outline has been given, and such the end of James Crabb. If the warrior who has fought the battles of his country, driven back her enemies from her gates, and by his heroic deeds brightened the pages of her history,—if the scholar who has discovered unexplored fields of knowledge, unlocked new treasures of science, and added, by his discoveries, to the comforts of his fellow-men,—if the statesman, who has advanced the prosperity of his country by the wisdom of his counsels and the suggestion of wholesome laws,—if men like these deserve well of their country, and the reverence of their fellow-men, surely the man who, instead of destroying men's lives, has helped to save their souls, who has promulgated the laws of God, taught his country-men to be loyal subjects, peaceful citizens, and useful Christians, who has brought down blessings upon his

country and her people by his prayers, and stirred up men
to works of beneficence and labours of love, by which God
has been glorified, and his kingdom upon earth extended,
deserves equal, if not greater honour from his fellow-men;
but in this fallen world its warriors, and scholars, and
statesmen seek for and obtain their honours here, whilst the
conquerors, the scholars, the statesmen of Jesus shall
receive theirs hereafter. It doth not indeed yet appear
what they shall be, but we know that when He whom they
loved and served shall appear, they also shall appear with
Him in glory. "They shall be mine in that day when I
make up my jewels, saith the Lord." Assembled worlds
shall then see them as God does; they shall acknowledge
their worth and ratify the sentence of heaven.

If, as we read, our Lord Jesus notes the trials, the persecutions, and the sufferings of His people,—if He remem-
bers the cups of cold water given in His name—if He
takes account of visits made to His sick disciples—if He
numbers the garments with which His people have clothed
His poor, and notices the bread they have dealt out to His
hungry ones, there is a record of what James Crabb,
through His grace, was permitted to do for His name's
sake. Methinks that in that day when He who was once
the man of sorrows shall come to be admired in all them
that believe, there will be a great throng amongst the
multitude whom no man can number of those who were
led by Mr. Crabb's faithful ministry to His feet. Should
it then be asked, "What are these which are arrayed in
white robes?" it will be answered, "These were the drunkards, the harlots, the infidels, the Sabbath-breakers, the
depraved from the courts and lanes of ·Wilton, and Rumsey, and Southampton,—the gipsies from the green lanes
of England's shires,—the trophies of James Crabb, "who

have washed their robes, and made them white in the blood of the Lamb."

Soon after Mr. Crabb's death a monument was raised over his remains at the expense of some of his many friends, and the following inscription, referring to the most striking events of his life, is inscribed upon it :

Sacred to the Memory

OF THE

REV. JAMES CRABB,

Of Southampton.

Born at Wilton, in the Year 1774.

By the Grace of God, in early life the subject of genuine Piety,
He devoted himself to the ministry of the Gospel ;
proclaiming its vital truths
And practising its holy duties, during the period of nearly
sixty years ;

Strong in faith, ardent in love to God and man,
Abundant in labours, and unselfish in his aims, aided also
By pecuniary assistance received from many in different parts
of the United Kingdom,
Who sympathised with his expansive benevolence, and approved
his zeal.

He, whilst actively employed as a Christian Pastor,
Either partly or entirely originated and sustained in the town
in which he lived,
Schools for the infant children of the poor ;
A Penitentiary for reclaiming the abandoned of the female sex ;
A Society for the religious instruction and social improvement
of the Gipsy Tribes,
Perpetuated in a School for their Children in Farnham,
Dorsetshire,
Combined with unwearied efforts for the Spiritual Benefit of
British and Foreign Sailors ;
Having served his own Generation, by the will of God,
he fell asleep,
In the full assurance of Hope,
On the 17th day of September, 1851.

Erected by the
Voluntary Contributions of Members of almost every Religious
Denomination,
To testify their profound respect for the Memory of one
Who, without professing to belong to any of the
numerous Sections
Of the Universal Church,
Was Beloved and Respected by them all.

The true worth of a man is seldom fully known till he dies. The blank he has left is then discovered, and thus it was in Mr. Crabb's case. When he was dead many regretted they had withheld from him their support; others that they had had so little sympathy with him in his labours and toils. The Corporation of Southampton, feeling the value of Mr. Crabb's labours amongst the people of that town, passed the following Resolutions, which were no less honourable to them than to the memory of Mr. Crabb:

AUDIT HOUSE, SOUTHAMPTON.

Monday, the 22nd of December, 1851.

At a Meeting of the Council of the Borough of Southampton, held this day at the Audit-house, or Council Chamber, in the said Borough, It was resolved unanimously:

" That the fee payable on the erection of the Monument in the Cemetery to the memory of the Rev. James Crabb be dispensed with; and, in connection with this Resolution, the Members of the Council desire to record their high appreciation not only of the private worth of that excellent man, but also of his unwearied and most disinterested efforts through a long series of years to improve the physical, moral, and spiritual condition of the inhabitants of the town; and the more so as those labours were especially and cheerfully devoted to the relief of the most destitute, the instruction of the most ignorant, and the reclamation of the most neglected of the population.

" That a copy of this Resolution be forwarded by the Town Clerk to the Friends of the Family."

CHAPTER XVI.

Mr. Crabb's want of learning.—Reflections on learning in connection with the ministry.—Conversion of Dairyman's Daughter under Mr. Crabb's preaching.—His preaching based on
evangelical truth.—Character of Mr. Crabb's preaching—to the
unconverted—to the converted.—His standard.—His spirit.—
His experience.—His mode of treating the failings of believers.
—His care of the " little ones."—Watched the results of his
preaching.—Remarks on worldly ministers.—The state of the
church.—The profession of the day.—Mr. Crabb's triumph
over all opposition.—Mr. Crabb's spirituality of mind.—His
abhorrence of covetousness.—Divisions in the church.—His
respect to the ordinances of man.—His assurance.—Quota-
tion from Jeremy Taylor touching the perfection of God's
servants.—Mr. Crabb's deep humility.

HAVING detailed the life and labours of Mr. Crabb, it
remains to notice some of the prominent features of his
ministerial and Christian character, which have not been,
or have been only briefly referred to in the preceding
pages.

We have already seen that Mr. Crabb was altogether
destitute of learning; but happily learning is not needed
to qualify a man to discover his fallen condition,—to
understand the covenant of grace,—to give utterance to
the language of prayer or make known the unsearchable
riches of Christ. Displays of oratory or rhetoric will no

more resuscitate dead souls than the minstrelsy of those who bewailed the dead maiden in the Gospel would awaken her to life. Had learning been essential to the successful promulgation of God's truth, that truth would not have been committed to men like James and Peter, nor would the Great Apostle of the Gentiles have failed, in his Epistles to Timothy and Titus, to point out so important a qualification for the Christian ministry. Judging from past experience it may be well doubted, whether, in any age of the church, learned ministers have been more successful than those who have had no learning —whether eloquence in our church has not been like the painted glass in the windows, which, though beautiful in itself, has served to darken or exclude the light; and whether, as Latimer has said, many have not been so learned as by their learning to have made many fools. "A plain experienced Christian," says Dr. Culverwell, in speaking of learned ministers, "by the help of a Bible, notwithstanding their auxiliary forces, will put a whole army of them to flight: *Surgunt indocti et rapiunt cœlum*, when they, in the mean time, do but *ornare Diabolum*." That learning, however, in its proper place, is a valuable auxiliary to the Gospel, especially in days like the present, when learning is so common, cannot be denied. Even the Apostle (like the Israelites who went down to the Philistines to sharpen their weapons against the day of battle,) made use of the learning of heathen schools to batter down the strongholds of the "wise," by instructing them through their own doctrines, and reproving them by their own sayings. But, alas! how often is learning, in scholastic garb, proud that it knows so much, whilst wisdom, in tattered garments, is humble because it knows so little. Happy are they who, like Nazianzen, can set no other value on learning than this—that they have something of worth to esteem as nothing for Christ! Learning thus estimated, and thus used, is sanctified; and, if the expression may be allowed, adorns the Gospel as the gold, the purple, the blue, and the scarlet did the breastplate of judgment. But although Mr. Crabb had no learning, he was not like many, who, having none themselves, and being too ignorant to discover its value, despise, or affect to despise it in others, and, like the cock in Æsop, prefer a barleycorn to a jewel He knew its value and regretted his want of it. His deficiencies made him "swift to hear and slow to speak," and taught him, as the Greek poet expresses it, to ascend downwards and descend upwards. Taking counsel of Him "in whom are hid all the treasures of wisdom and knowledge," He gave him a mouth and wisdom—that Divine wisdom which is not to be acquired in the halls of learning, or the schools of philosophy—which is not of "the earth, earthy;" but teaches a man "to find the knowledge of God," and makes him not only "wise unto salvation," but "wise to win souls" to Christ. Thus assisted, and thus instructed, he laboured—strong in the Lord and in the power of His might, and made it manifest, both in word and in deed, that he was called of God to labour in His vineyard, as he of old, whose rod "brought forth buds, bloomed blossoms, and yielded almonds," or as they who "being scattered abroad went everywhere preaching the word."

Mr. Crabb's preaching was of a very earnest and energetic character. He was a Boanerges in the pulpit, and many a stout-hearted sinner has quailed under his exhibitions of sin and the terrors of the wrath to come; but at the same time he had a winning and touching way of setting forth the love of Christ, and his willingness to save the vilest. He knew that men were not to be frightened or driven, but drawn to Christ, and what he records in some of his Diaries that he wept over the people, and that they—even the vilest—wept as he preached, is literally true. It is not generally known that he was the honoured instrument of bringing Elizabeth Wallbridge (better known as the Dairyman's daughter) to a know-ledge of Christ. She was then a servant in a family residing near the Gate in Southampton, and having been persuaded by two of her fellow servants to accompany them on a week day evening to hear Mr. Crabb, who was to preach in a licensed room in Hanover-buildings, she went, little knowing that her footsteps were that night directed by Divine mercy, and that she was going forth to meet Him who had loved her with an everlasting love, and was about to draw her by His spirit to Himself. She was at that time, as she has herself testified, of a vain and worldly spirit; but the word preached that night went home to her heart, and was, through Him with whom nothing is too hard, effectual to awaken her to a sense of her lost condition as a sinner, and her need of deliverance from it. Having been brought into much soul conflict, she went the next time Mr. Crabb preached in Southampton, to hear him, and his sermon then com-pleted the work which had been begun in her soul. God spoke to her by His spirit, and revealed to her His glory in the face of Jesus. At His cross, in deep abasement, she laid down her sins; and at his gracious hands received that righteousness "which is unto all and upon all them that believe." The change which had been thus wrought in her is recorded in the letters published by Mr. Legh Richmond in his exquisite narrative of her life; but there

is an earlier letter which she wrote to her brother, telling
him what God had done for her, and expressive of the
great love she felt for Mr. Crabb, as her spiritual father,
which Mr. Richmond never saw.

It bears date Southampton, March 3rd, 1796, and is as
follows :

" MY DEAR BROTHER,—I received your kind letter of
2nd instant, and you may think what a transport of joy
I felt to receive such an affectionate letter from a brother
I had so little regarded since he had left the world and
me.   You may well say what great joy it gave you to hear
I was converted to God—but are you the only one ?   No.
My dear brother, I think what shouting and rejoicing
there was with the angels of God in heaven, that are
around the throne, and continually cry, ' Worthy the
Lamb of God that was slain, to receive all glory, and
honour, and praise.'   And blessed be God, who hath
showed strength with his hand, and with his holy arm
hath gotten himself the victory !

   * * * * *

" It was when I was sitting under that delightful man,
Mr. Crabb, that the Lord opened my eyes ; it was the second
time that I heard him.   And on Sunday last, in the morning, I was standing at the window, and he came past, and
when I saw him my heart leaped within me for joy ; for I
believed him to be commissioned from the Most High God
to preach the Gospel of salvation and peace to all that will
hear it . . . And now, my dear brother, as I have no money
with me, I beg you will apply to my dear mother for six
guineas of my money, and give them to Mr. Crabb, and
tell him it is a free gift of a poor needy creature, who
has been to the Lamb of God, naked and destitute of
everything ; and then, when He saw my wretched condi-

tion, with what tender compassion did He look down upon me, and sprinkle me with His blood, and give me the whole armour of God, the shield of faith, the helmet of salvation, and the breastplate of righteousness ... My dear brother, buy Mr. Crabb a very large Bible, that when he looks upon it he may bless his God, and think what good he hath done for my poor soul, through the gracious influence of the Spirit ... Pray excuse this, and write as soon as you conveniently can. Adieu, dear brother.

"ELIZABETH WALLBRIDGE."

Mr. Crabb was often requested by his friends to make known the inaccuracies which exist in Mr. Legh Richmond's narrative with reference to the conversion of this eminent saint; but Mr. Crabb, who did not seek the honour that cometh from man, in a letter written to a friend, said, "I have felt very unwilling to correct these inaccuracies, lest I should in any measure lessen the importance and value of the tract." He further observed, "I lost sight of her myself for several years, but one day a friend came to me and said, 'I have a guinea sent to me by the brother of Elizabeth Wallbridge for you. It comes from her death-bed, and she desires your acceptance of it as a small token of Christian love to you, as the instrument of her conversion.' I valued the manner in which it was done, and received the token as the grateful gift of a dying Christian. I love her memory, and rejoice that the memoir has been the instrument of converting and comforting thousands of my poor fellow-sinners; and I most fervently pray that it may long continue to be a blessing to the Church and the world." Well may we say, in reading this letter, "He giveth grace to the humble."

But Mr. Crabb was not only eminently useful in

preaching to the unconverted, but was, as he who writes this, and many others can testify, a helper of the joy of those who, through grace, have believed. Even so early as the year 1796, at a time when he was broken down by illness, and almost incapable of standing in the pulpit, I find this affecting record in his Diary: " Sunday, 15th ——. At nine o'clock, set off for Shaftesbury, to preach for a dear friend, a Calvinist minister, now quite an invalid. Many years ago, when he used to be at my father's house, I had many serious impressions under him. I had great desire to be a minister of Christ when he used to dandle me on his knee. Lord, what hast Thou done! and what art Thou now doing in and by the weakest of thy creatures! I am a wonder to myself. What hast Thou called me unto! O that I were more faithful and devoted to Thee! In the morning I preached from Psalm lxvii. 18. Mr. Marchant was greatly affected under my preaching, and wept much. Although a man of great knowledge, and a good theologian, he seemed to sit at the feet of one who knew nothing. O Lord, what a mercy it is that I know Christ! Oh, to know more of Him, and that day by day ! "

One of the great secrets of Mr. Crabb's success as a preacher was, that his preaching, which was the fruit of his prayers, was based on evangelical truth ; in other words, on the teaching of our Lord and his apostles. Having believed, he spoke, and when he spoke he could truly say, as a matter of experience—for his religion was not form, but life—" that which we have *heard,* and which we have *seen* with our eyes, which we have *looked upon,* and our hands have *handled* of the word of God, declare we unto you." He did not, therefore, preach as some men do, from the head, but from the heart ; he did not deal with abstractions, but realities—with solemn certainties and not with speculations.

There was a great discrimination in his mode of setting forth the truth. He had learnt in a spiritual sense that " the fitches are not threshed with a threshing instrument, nor a cart-wheel turned about upon the cummin; that the fitches are beaten out with a staff, and the cummin with a rod, and that bread corn is bruised," Isa. xxviii. 27. He, therefore, never generalized, but particularized. He did not address men dead in trespasses and sins, as men spiritually alive and risen with Christ. Knowing that without faith there can be no love, and that without love there can be no filial obedience, he began as our Lord himself did with Nicodemus—with the great and fundamental truth, that " except a man be born again, he cannot see the kingdom of God." Having shown the sinner his lost state, he led him to the cross of Jesus as his only refuge, bade him look to His blood as that by which alone he could " obtain redemption, even the forgiveness of sin," and to his obedience for that righteousness which is " unto all and upon all them that believe." He did not say to the convinced sinner, " Hear the Church," for he knew as Musculus well expresses it, that " Any man may be in the body of Christ,—that is, the church—and live by the spirit of Christ in any corner of the earth, if he do truly believe in Him; yea, although he never heard or understood a letter of the name of the Church of Rome;" or it may be added, the Church of England, or any other church. He knew, moreover, as the same learned divine has said " that the true church is the company and fellowship of the true, faithful, holy, and elect, standing in faith, hope, love, and the spirit of Christ;" and that the church can know nothing, except through the word, by the teaching of the Spirit. He therefore directed the inquiring sinner to the word itself, which, testifying of Jesus, is able, through that teaching, to make a man, without the aid of tradition, wise unto salvation, through faith in Christ Jesus, and by which the man of God is *thoroughly furnished* unto *all* good works.*

* In a day like the present, when men would throw contempt on the Word of God, the writer is tempted to quote, at length, a passage with reference to the Bible from the work of a divine, who, notwithstanding his faults and want of education, was one of the most extraordinary and gifted men of his age, and whose writings, notwithstanding the dogmatism and bitterness with which they abound, and their lack of preceptive teaching, contain a large body of valuable divinity. " I have," he says, " sometimes thought, that a nation must be truly blessed, if it were governed by no other laws than those of that blessed book. It is so complete a system, that nothing can be added to it or taken from it. It contains every thing needful to be known and done. It affords a *copy* for a king, Deut. xvii. 18, and a *rule* for a subject. It gives instruction and counsel to a senate, authority and direction for a magistrate. It cautions a witness, requires an impartial verdict of a jury, and furnishes the judge with his sentence. It sets the husband as lord of the household, and the wife as mistress of the table : tells *him* how to rule, and *her* how to manage. It entails honour to parents, and enjoins obedience to children. It prescribes and limits the sway of the sovereign, the rule of the ruler, and the authority of the master, commands the subject to honour, and the servant to obey ; and promises the blessing and protection of its Author to all who walk by its rules. It gives directions for weddings, and for burials ; regulates *feasts* and *fasts*, mournings and rejoicings ; and orders labour for the day, and rest for the night. It promises food and raiment, and limits the use of both. It points out a faithful and an eternal *Guardian* to the departing husband and father ; tells him with whom to leave his fatherless children, and in whom his widow is to trust, Jer. xlix. 11 ; and promises a father to the former, and a husband to the latter. It teaches a man how to

Mr. Crabb's mode of preaching to believers was no less distinguished by its apostolic standard, for whilst he did not

set his house in order, and how to make his will. It appoints a dowry for the wife, entails the right of the first-born, and shows how the younger branches shall be left : it defends the rights of all ; and reveals vengeance to every defrauder, over-reacher, or oppressor. It is the first book, the best book, and the oldest book in all the world. It contains the choicest matter, gives the best instruction, and affords the greatest pleasure and satisfaction, that ever was revealed. It contains the best laws and profoundest mysteries that ever were penned. It brings the best of tidings, and affords the best of comfort, to the inquiring and disconsolate. It exhibits life and immortality from everlasting, and shows the way to eternal glory. It is a brief recital of all that is passed, and a certain prediction of all that is to come. It settles all matters in debate, resolves all doubts, and eases the mind and conscience of all their scruples. It reveals the only living and true God, and shows the way to him ; it sets aside all other gods, and describes the vanity of them, and of all that trust in them. In short, it is a book of law, to show right and wrong ; a book of wisdom, that condemns all folly, and makes the foolish wise ; a book of truth, that detects all lies, and confutes all errors ; and a book of life, that gives life, and shows the way from everlasting death. It is the most compendious book in all the world ; the most ancient, authentic, and the most entertaining history, that ever was published. It contains the most ancient antiquities, strange events, wonderful occurrences, heroic deeds, and unparalleled wars. It describes the celestial, terrestrial, and infernal worlds ; and the origin of the angelic myriads, human tribes, and devilish legions. It will instruct the most accomplished mechanic, and the profoundest artist ; it will teach the best rhetorician, and exercise every power of the most skilful arithmetician, Rev. xiii. 18 ; puzzle the wisest anatomist, and exercise the nicest critic. It corrects the vain philosopher, and confutes the wise astronomer ; it exposes the subtle sophist, and makes diviners mad. It is a complete code of laws, a perfect body of divinity, an unequalled narrative, a book of lives, a book of travels, and a book of voyages. It is the best *covenant* that preach to the unconverted as to those who were converted, he did not preach to the converted as to those who needed conversion, but as unto spiritual. He knew that amongst the Lord's people there were mourners to be comforted— the timid to be encouraged—the tempted to be succoured —the careless to be reproved—the strong to be nourished and the weak and sickly to be supported, and that he was the honoured channel through which the Lord himself conveyed messages to many who Sabbath after Sabbath came up to the sanctuary to hear what the Lord their God had to say to them in answer to their prayers. His aim, therefore, through help obtained of God, was so to divide the word as to give to all " their portion of meat in due season."

His standard (which was founded on that of the Wesleyan school) was high and holy. He never insulted the Lord, or disgraced the Gospel by calling that Christianity which is but its counterfeit, neither did he set gifts in the

---

ever was agreed on, the best *deed* that ever was sealed, the best *evidence* that ever was produced, the best *will* that ever was made, and the best *testament* that ever was signed. To understand it, is to be wise indeed ; to be ignorant of it, is to be destitute of wisdom. It is the King's best *copy*, the magistrate's best *rule*, the housewife's best *guide*, the servant's best *directory*, and the young man's best *companion*. It is the schoolboy's *spelling-book*, and the learned man's *master-piece*. It contains a choice *grammar* for a novice, and a profound *mystery* for a sage. It is the ignorant man's dictionary, and the wise man's directory. It affords knowledge of witty inventions for the *humorous*, and dark sayings for the *grave* ; and is its own interpreter. It encourages the wise, the warrior, the swift, and the overcomer ; and promises an eternal reward to the excellent, the conqueror, the winner, and the prevalent. And that which crowns all is, that the Author is without partiality, and without hypocrisy ; in whom is no variableness, or shadow of turning."—*Huntington's Works*, vol. i. 536.

place of grace, or morality in the place of godliness. He had a great horror of preaching mere doctrines to the exclusion of the precepts of the Gospel. He did not treat the saints of God as spiritual automatons, acted upon by secret impulses, but as responsible stewards of the manifold grace of God—as earthen vessels that needed to beware of falls. Brought into the relationship of children, and admitted to the privileges which stand connected with it, he urged upon them the duties of mortification and self-denial—of giving all diligence—of growing in grace—of adding to their faith the Christian graces—of striving and resisting—of not grieving the Spirit, and of judging themselves lest they should be judged of the Lord, and being judged by Him, should be chastened. Nor did he forget to press upon them that they, and they alone, were the Lord's witnesses, the reflection of his glory, the personifications of his truth, and that there was no other way of showing forth his praises, and manifesting that he had called them to his kingdom and glory, than by a holy, watchful, prayerful walk and conversation. He did not, however, set them to work in their own strength, for he knew, as evangelically expressed in the collect of the Church of England, that in all the works of Christian men they have need of grace to prevent, or go before, and grace to follow them : and therefore he directed the believing people of God to rest on the Holy Ghost as the great teacher of the church, the Divine testifier of Jesus by whom alone they could be " guided into all truth," enlightened, strengthened, and sanctified.*

* Dr. Samuel Bolton, in his " Dead Saint Speaking," thus strikingly speaks of good works, a subject too often lost sight of by some, and misplaced by others. " Are good works," he asks,

He never lost sight of the great truth, that if a man be in Christ, he is a new creature; and he looked for and expected to see its actings in that newness of life, which is its unfailing concomitant. His great master, Wesley, has so beautifully delineated the portraiture of the new creature that the Christian reader, though he may have admired it before, will perhaps not regret to have it once more set before him. Speaking of a man in Christ, he says :

" First, his judgments are new ; his judgment of himself, of happiness, of holiness. He judges himself to be

" good for nothing, because not good to justify ?" We say works are necessary,

I. In respect of God.
II. In respect of ourselves.
III. In respect of others.

I. In respect of God.

1. To show our obedience.
2. To glorify his name.
3. To testify our thankfulness.
4. To beautify his gospel.

II. In respect of ourselves.

1. To make our calling and election sure.
2. To declare our sincerity.
3. To procure mercy.

III. In respect of others.

1. To refresh the bowels of the saints.
2. For example of virtue.
3. To stop the mouths of wicked men, who would else take occasion to blaspheme the gospel, and speak evil of profession.
4. To win others.

" Good works," he adds, " are the breath, τὸ πνεῦμα, of faith, as the word in *James* signifies ; and as the body without breath is dead, so *faith without works is dead also*."—*Royalties of Faith*, p. 180.

altogether fallen short of the glorious image of God; to have no good thing abiding in him, but all that is corrupt and abominable : in a word, to be wholly earthly, sensual, and devilish, a motley mixture of beast and devil. Thus, by the grace of God in Christ, I judge of myself. Therefore I am in this respect a new creature.

" Again, his judgment concerning happiness is new. He would as soon expect to dig it out of the earth, as to find it in riches, honour, pleasure (so called), or indeed in the enjoyment of any creature. He knows there can be no happiness on earth, but in the enjoyment of God, and in the foretaste of those rivers of pleasure which flow at His right hand for evermore. Thus, by the grace of God in Christ, I judge of happiness. Therefore I am in this respect a new creature.

" Yet again, his judgment concerning holiness is new. He no longer judges it to be an outward thing; to consist either in doing no harm, in doing good, or in using the ordinances of God. He sees it is the life of God in the soul; the image of God fresh stamped on the heart; an entire renewal of the mind in every temper and thought, after the likeness of Him that created it. Thus, by the grace of God in Christ, I judge of holiness. Therefore I am in this respect a new creature.

" Secondly, his designs are new. It is the design of his life, not to heap up treasures upon earth, not to gain the praise of men, not to indulge the desires of the flesh, the desires of the eye, or the pride of life : but to regain the image of God, to have the life of God again planted in his soul, and to be renewed after his likeness in righteousness and all true holiness. This, by the grace of God in Christ, is the design of my life. Therefore I am in this respect a new creature.

" Thirdly, his desires are new, and indeed the whole train of his passions and inclinations ; they are no longer fixed on earthly things; they are now set on the things of heaven. His love and joy and hope, his sorrow and fear, have all respect to things above : they all point heavenward. Where his treasure is, there is his heart also.—I dare not say I am a new creature in this respect, for other desires often arise in my heart : but they do not reign, I put them all under my feet through Christ which strengtheneth me; therefore, I believe that He is creating me anew in this also, and that He has begun, though not finished his work.

" Fourthly, his conversation is new. It is *always seasoned with salt, and fit to minister grace to the hearers.* So is mine, by the grace of God in Christ; therefore, I am in this respect a new creature.

" Fifthly, his actions are new. The tenor of his life singly points at the glory of God ; all his substance and time are devoted thereto: *whether he eats or drinks, or whatever he does,* it either springs from, or leads to the love of God and man. Such, by the grace of God in Christ, is the tenor of my life ; therefore, in this respect, I am a new creature."

And such was the standard of Mr. Crabb. But whether Mr. Crabb, as a minister, reproved, exhorted, or rebuked, he did it in a spirit of tenderness and love. In the language of Bishop Reynolds :

" His care of men's souls made him take upon himself every man's affection, and accommodate himself to every man's temper ; that he might not offend the weak, nor exasperate the mighty, nor dishearten the beginner, nor affright those who were without from coming in ; but be all in all unto their salvation. The same love," adds that eminent divine, "is due unto all, but the same method of cure is not requisite for all : with some, love travaileth in pain ; with others, it rejoiceth in hope ; some it laboureth to edify, and others it feareth to offend ; unto the weak it stoopeth ; unto the strong it raiseth itself ; unto some it is compassionate, to others severe ; to some an enemy, to all a mother. But all this it doth, not by belying the truth, but by pitying the sinner. It is not the wisdom of the flesh, nor to be learned of men ; the Scripture alone is able to make the man of God wise unto the work of salvation."

Mr. Crabb had learnt by experience, that where weariness begins, devotion ends ; and therefore he did not generally preach long sermons, which too often, like overfeathered arrows, shoot beyond their mark. Would that some ministers considered this as they ought. How often, after they have convinced men's judgments, probed their consciences, and touched their hearts, not satisfied to leave the success to God, who alone can make the word effectual, they run on as though they thought the success of their preaching depended on much speaking, and thus weary their hearers, destroy the feelings they have awakened, and wear out the impression they have made.

Mr. Crabb was a minister of much experience, and possessed a large stock of what is called practical divinity. He had been a great observer of the Lord's dealings with himself and others ; and having by the past of his life learnt something for the improvement of the future, he was enabled to counsel, instruct, and comfort others by what he had himself learnt. In this consists the difference between a mere notional and an experimental minister. The former can discourse of things he never realised or felt, whilst the other has learnt them experi-

mentally in the school of suffering and trial. The
former can dip his pen in the word, but the other can
not only dip his pen there, but in his heart also. There
is a story somewhere in ancient writ which will serve to
illustrate this distinction. A king having lost his only
son, and being in deep affliction, his courtiers endeavoured
to console him by every topic they could urge; but
nothing they could say went home to his heart, or afforded
him the slightest comfort. At length a poor widow,
who, like him, had lost an only son, approached him
bathed in tears, and spoke so sweetly in the language of
sympathy, as to alleviate in some degree the sorrow that
pressed upon his heart. Touched by her consolatory
words, he turned to his courtiers and said, " I have
received more comfort from the words of this poor woman
than from all your fine speeches and studied words, and
for this reason, that she has experienced the sorrows I
feel, and knows how to comfort me with the comforts
she herself has found."

But although Mr. Crabb had much general experience
in the spiritual life, few excelled him in his felicitous mode
of administering comfort to tried and tempted believers,
or those who had been made desolate by the hand of
affliction. He had all his life been accustomed to such
cases, and for such he had a stock of balm from the
garden of Gilead ever ready, which he knew well how to
apply; so that, as Isaiah was instructed, to "take a lump
of figs and lay it for a plaster on the boil, and he shall
recover," he was often instructed by the same gracious
Teacher how to speak to the troubled, and to bind up the
broken in heart.

In the course of his ministry he had seen—and who
that has mingled with the church of God has not?—

much of the failings, inconsistencies, and mistakes of
the Lord's people; but knowing something of the wiles
of Satan and the power of temptation, and that great
corruptions are often mingled with much grace, he covered
their defects with the mantle of love, looked on their
patience rather than their impatience, their meekness
rather than their roughness, their submission rather than
their murmurings, and their labours of love rather than
their short-comings. He knew that the Lord sometimes
leaves a believer to himself to prove or humble him, and
that in such seasons, like David or Peter, in an unwatchful
moment he may, without losing his interest in Christ,
fall into sin. Whilst others might brand such an one as
a reprobate or castaway, and cry out, like those who stood
around Eutychus when he fell from the third loft, "he
is dead," Mr. Crabb looked upon him with compassion,
and, to borrow an illustration from the learned Weemse,
like Paul embraced him in his arms, and said, "He is not
dead, his life is in him."

There was also another trait in Mr. Crabb's character
which deserves to be recorded, and that was his peculiar
attention to the "little ones" of the Lord's flock, who
are so often discouraged by injudicious treatment, and
saddened by those who have not learnt to bear the
infirmities of the weak. In social gatherings of the Lord's
people for prayer and converse over the word, if one of
those "little ones" asked a question or made a remark—
perhaps not very relevant or wise,—Mr. Crabb did not let
it pass in silence, or answer it with a repulsive look; but
remembering the Lord's concern for such, and his rebuke
of those who would have kept them back from him, he
was kind and condescending to the feeblest and weakest,
bore with their ignorance and mistakes, encouraged their

inquiries, and was ready to impart to them the simplest instruction, caring not to please himself so that he did not offend them.

Mr. Crabb, as one of the Lord's sowers, was not content to sow the "seed of the kingdom" without watching its progress, and ascertaining whether it was productive of fruit. He felt a deep concern for the souls of his people; and like his Master, who, after He had preached to his disciples, inquired of them, "Understand ye what ye have heard," he made the like inquiry of his hearers, watched over them as one who must give account, marked their progress or declension in the ways of God, and exhorted them as a father doth his children. Thus he not only learnt the defects and deficiencies of his ministry, but the spiritual condition of his people, acquired a great knowledge of character, and in conversation with well instructed Christians learnt much which probably he would never otherwise have known. And this was as it ever should be with one who claims to fill the pastoral office. The Apostle could say to the people under his charge, "What is our hope, or joy, or crown of rejoicing? Are not even ye in the presence of our Lord Jesus Christ at His coming?" But how can any minister say this if he know not the people amongst whom he labours, and is wholly ignorant of their spiritual state? Instead of being his hope, or joy, or crown of rejoicing in the great day of his Lord's appearing, he may find that not only has he no account to give of them, but that they are his disgrace and shame; and that instead of building up in his ministry "gold, silver, and precious stones," he has built only "wood, hay, and stubble, and he himself is saved as by fire."

But whilst Mr. Crabb felt it a duty to ascertain the

spiritual state of his people by visitation, he never joined
in any of their festivities, or went where he was to fill the
character of a gentleman, and not that of a Christian minister; for he knew that on such occasions what is of the flesh
has generally the ascendancy; that watchfulness and circum-
spection are too often laid aside; that the high and holy
principles of self-denial and separation from the world
promulgated in the pulpit are generally lost sight of; and
it is frequently discovered that the minister has not yet
attained what he would have others to practise, and
possesses the corruptions which he condemns in his
people. "The desire," says that man of God, Cecil, "to be
thought a man who has kept good company strikes at the
root of that *rough work*—the bringing of God into his
own world. To talk of a Creator, Preserver, and Redeemer is an outrage on the feelings of most companies."
Happy indeed would it be for ministers in general if in
these days of worldliness, when the church has corrupted
its manners by assimilating them to those of the world,
and by worldly conformity, they would ponder well these
words, and were seen less in the circles of fashion, where
no distinction is made between the church and the world.
By being present at such assemblies the minister sanc-
tions what the word of God condemns; and for him to
" wind up " such meetings with that word and by prayer,
is practically to deny the Lord Jesus, to delude souls, to
consecrate "the lust of the flesh, the lust of the eye, and
the pride of life;" and to declare that what God has put
asunder may be joined together.

We live in days when the church and the world seem
to have made mutual concessions. The world has surrendered some of its grossness—the church some of its spirituality : the world has ascended one step higher, and the

church descended many steps lower, that they may embrace each other. There is, doubtless, much bustle and stir—many are up and doing—but is not much of it the activity of the head and not of the heart—the influence of feeling, and not of principle—an impulse from without, and not from the Spirit? Great exertions are made, but is there not little prayer? Much dependence is placed on man, but is there not little trust in the Lord? Society itself begins to feel the influence of new principles, founded on expediency or a false charity. Hence it is, that the children of this world, decked with the garb of godliness, are embraced as the children of light : and the children of light, dressed out in the garments of this world, are often undistinguishable from those who are " of the earth, earthy." Hence also, it comes to pass, that a man is now measured, in so-called Christian society, not by the grace he possesses, but by his equipage; not because he is one with Christ, but because he is one with the great, the gay, and the proud, "whom they call, happy." The rich and the titled are courted, but the Lord's precious ones are often neglected and passed over. The days which were foretold seem to have come upon us. Men are "lovers of their own selves," yet, "having a form of godliness" — "covetous, boasters, proud, despisers of those that are good, lovers of pleasures more than lovers of God," yet all —all having the "form of godliness;" but let Satan put the suitable temptation in the way of these formalists, and they become "spectacles to angels and to men." Their true characters may be illustrated by a story which Lucian, in his "Resuscitated Philosophers," relates of an Egyptian king. Being possessed of a number of apes, he had them trained from their earliest age to dance with considerable agility. Having dressed them in masks and purple robes, he made them exercise their skill in the presence of the great people who came to his court, and who, not knowing they were apes, but taking them for men, wondered how the king came to have such nimble little men in his service; but a shrewd individual who had been admitted to see their performances, had the sagacity to discover that they were apes and not men, and being invited on a grand occasion to see them, in the midst of their performances, scattered amongst them a handful of nuts, which they no sooner spied than they left off dancing, fell to scrambling and fighting, tore one another's fine clothes, and, to the mortification of the king, the beholders discovered that they were nothing but apes. Such are the characters whom I have described; they have the appearance of Christians, speak the language of Canaan, and pass for a time as saints; but as soon as the god of this world scatters amongst them the nuts of riches, honours, and worldly distinctions, they are found not to be Christians, but spiritual apes.

No man who devoted himself to the Lord's service as Mr. Crabb did, could, unless the offence of the cross had ceased, expect to escape persecution, and we have seen from the foregoing pages that he, like his forerunners, was called to suffer and endure; and this is not to be wondered at, for had not Satan hindered and the world frowned, it might have been doubted whether he was sent of God. Some of his enemies, hoping to hinder his usefulness, exhumed the misfortunes of his early life; but "none of these things moved him," for he could say, with better reason than Diogenes did when he was vilified, "They vilify me, yet I am not vilified, for I am not the man they take me for." In tribulations like these he rejoiced, for he was delivered from the woe denounced by

L 2

his Master—"Woe unto you when all men speak well of you." His concern for souls led him to engage in such astonishing labours, that men said of him, as they said of his Master, "He is mad and hath a devil;" but it was with him as it was with Democritus, when his fellow-citizens declared him to be mad, and begged of Hippocrates to cure him;—that physician pronounced all the city mad but him.

But Mr. Crabb did not stand alone in bearing the reproach of those who had no sympathy with him in his labours. When the late General Orde, who was devotedly attached to him, at his request laid the foundation-stone of the Infant School at Kingsland (a circumstance which ought to have been mentioned in a former page), he had to bear not only the ridicule of many professing Christians, but the contumely of some of the newspapers of the day, because he addressed the persons assembled on that occasion from a wagon. That gallant officer, however, was not ashamed of Christ, and esteemed it an honour to participate with Mr. Crabb in reproach for His sake whom they both loved, and for the advancement of whose glory they both laboured in their respective spheres. General Orde is now numbered with those who sleep in Jesus. May they by whom he was vilified have no more reason on the day when the Lord shall come to be admired in all them that believe, to dread His presence, than that devoted man of God will then have in the retrospect of *that* for which he was vilified and reproached by them.

That the Lord should permit his most valuable servants to be thus assailed and persecuted, is one of those mysterious things which the world cannot understand, and under which the saints themselves have need to be exhorted to be patient. St. Paul, speaking of himself and his fellow labourers, could say, "Being reviled, we bless; being persecuted, we suffer it; being defamed, we entreat;" and thus, revilings, persecutions, and defamations, were, by the mercy of God, the means of bringing out those graces by which He was glorified, and the exhibition of which has served in all ages of the church to show what Divine grace can enable the Lord's people to do, to bear, and to suffer; and thus it was with Mr. Crabb, for what was designed to his hurt turned to his profit, by bringing him to deeper humiliation before God, to more prayerful self-examination, and a more circumspect walk before his fellow-men. The Lord dealt very graciously with him, in standing " by him in all his tribulations, and strengthening him," and causing him to rest on the promise made to Jacob of old, " I will make thee a new, sharp threshing instrument having teeth; thou shalt thresh the mountains, and beat them small, and shalt make the hills as chaff; thou shalt fan them and the wind shall carry them away, and the whirlwind shall scatter them, and thou shalt rejoice in the Lord and glory in the Holy One of Israel." By the aboundings of His grace, he was enabled to live down all opposition, and " put to silence the ignorance of foolish men." And so it ever has been and shall be with the Lord's people : " no weapon that is formed against them shall prosper, and every tongue that shall rise against them in judgment they shall condemn."

Mr. Crabb was a man of whom it may be truly said, his conversation was in heaven. " The things of the Spirit" were those with which he was daily occupied. " Few men," as his daughter-in-law observed to me, " had less *idle words*." He viewed everything in the light of Divine truth, and aimed to do all he did as in the prospect of eternity. Having presented himself to God "a living

sacrifice," he felt that he was no longer his own, and that
to waste his time, his talents, or his influence, was to waste
what belonged to God. The value of every engagement and
employment was estimated by him in proportion as it was
likely to promote the glory of God, and the one object for
which alone he lived—the salvation of his fellow-men.
Though much occupied in duties, he did not rest in them,
but prized them in proportion as he met the Lord in them.
He gathered up the fragments of everything spiritual,
and profited as well by the sins of other men as his
own.

Much of his success—and it was great—was the fruit
of earnest and continual prayer. His desire was, that the
work without should keep pace with the work within, a
desire not easily accomplished, and in the attainment of
which miserable failures are often experienced. As one of
the habits of his life, he never undertook or engaged in
any affair or business, however trifling it might appear in
the eyes of others, without seeking counsel of Him with
whom there are no trifles; for with the poet, he felt that

> " Naught is great,
> Nor small with God—for none but He can make
> An atom indivisible, and none
> But He can make a world."

It was often said of him, that he lived in the precincts of
the eternal world, and certainly the key of heaven's treasury, that key *quâ Dei penetralia aperiuntur*, and which
the Lord had committed to him (as he does to each of His
believing people), was never rusty for want of use.

Living thus near to Him whom his soul loved, he saw
more of the bright unveilings of His face, heard more of
the whispers of his voice, and knew more of His secrets,

than those who lived at a greater distance from Him. Fixing his eyes continually on Him, he was changed into the same image from glory to glory, and, in like manner, as the sun's rays are in part absorbed by the earth, in part reflected back, and in part refracted in every direction, so the glory which shone into his soul was in part absorbed there to his own comfort, part was reflected back in praise, and the other part refracted on every side in benevolence to his fellow-men.

Another striking feature of Mr. Crabb's character was his unbounded abhorrence of covetousness, which Bolton has well called the *cut-throat of grace.* Struggling, as he did, all his life to get money for the Lord's cause, he had seen what covetousness is in all its selfish and hateful developments. The love of money or the things of this world was not one of his failings. " He looked," to quote the words of Lockyer, " with a very piercing eye upon everything ; through pearls and through gold, through the hardest thing to be pierced, and found out exactly what they were, and called them as they are—corruptible things." Jehovah Jireh was his motto. He served the Lord, and looked to Him for his reward, knowing that He would not suffer him to want long, though he might try his faith by permitting him to seem to want, as he did in the days referred to in a former page, when " no man gave unto him," and he was left to satisfy the cravings of hunger with the wild fruit of the hedges. How, with the pittance he received from his chapel, considering the extreme generosity of his nature, which rendered it impossible for him to meet with a case of distress without relieving it, he contrived to bring up and educate his family has often been a surprise to many. It is supposed, upon a moderate calculation, that from the time of his coming to Southampton to the termination of his ministry, he received upwards of £20,000 for charitable uses; and of this he was a faithful steward. He never saved a shilling; and during the last ten years of his life, so long as he had an interest in the profits of the school carried on by his two sons, he spent by far the greater proportion of what he received, in his Master's cause; but his children were thus mercifully preserved from the curse of inheriting a portion which belonged to the church of God, and which ought to have been applied to the relief of God's poor, and the advancement of His cause in the world. He left nothing behind for moths to corrupt or thieves to steal,—his treasure was in heaven.

There was nothing which Mr. Crabb felt more deeply, or upon which he expressed himself more strongly, than the divisions in the church of God. That men should differ in externals and circumstantials is not to be wondered at; but that men, professing to be disciples of Jesus, children of the "one family," should "bite and devour one another," and deal out invective and "railing accusations" against their brethren, filled his heart with sorrow. Love, and not uniformity of worship or conformity of opinion, is the true test of *brotherhood,* the only tie which binds heart to heart. Agreement of opinion in those things with respect to which God has not enjoined it, is not to be expected; nor did Mr. Crabb spend his time in endeavours to promote it, for it is contrary to man's fallen nature, to experience, and the Word of God.

> " There is no similitude in Nature that owneth not also to a
>   difference ;
>   Yea, no two berries are alike, though twins upon one stem ;
>   No drop in the ocean, no pebble on the beach, no leaf in the
>   forest hath its counterpart ;

No mind in its dwelling of mortality, no spirit in the world
    unseen ;
And, therefore, since capacity and essence differ alike with
    accident,
None but a bigot partizan will hope for impossible unity."

Such being the Catholic spirit of Mr. Crabb, he was
ever ready to make any sacrifice but that of principle to
secure unity and promote peace. When he lived at Rumsey, in days when dissent was classed by many with trea-
son, his blameless life and extraordinary labours amongst
the poor attracted the notice of the Rev. Daniel Williams,
the rector of the parish, who accosted him one day with the
inquiry, whether he paid Easter offerings, and upon being
answered in the affirmative, he good-humouredly remarked,
" Brother Crabb, parson should not eat parson, and I beg
you will not pay them again." But Mr. Crabb felt that
they were his due; and desiring to fulfil the injunction,
" render to *all* their dues ; tribute to whom tribute is due,
and custom to whom custom," he continued to pay them.
In like manner he paid tithes and church-rates, remembering Him who left His disciples an example that they
should follow in His footsteps, and who, rather than give
offence, worked a miracle, that He and His disciples might
be enabled to pay a tax, though exacted by a corrupt
government. Besides, as an honest man, he felt bound to
pay every lawful imposition, for he knew that the value of
every tax upon property is not only taken into consideration upon its purchase, but the amount calculated upon
the creation of every tenancy, so that in fact it is not the
tenant who *bears* these charges, though he pays them, but
the owner who took them into account upon his purchase,
and who, did they not exist, would obtain a larger price
and a higher rent for his property.

Few men ever attained to a higher degree of assurance, or enjoyed greater peace with God, than did Mr. Crabb; but he did not attain this greatest of all spiritual blessings so easily as some *appear* to do. It was the fruit of long waiting upon God, and fidelity to Him. "If a man love me," says our Lord, "he will keep my words; and my Father will love him, and we will come unto him, and make our abode with him," from which it is manifest that it is in the pathway of obedient walking that God reveals himself to his children, and that it is to him that ordereth his conversation aright He shows His salvation. "Thou meetest him," says the prophet, "that rejoiceth and worketh righteousness; those that remember Thee in Thy ways:" truths which Mr. Crabb had fully realised in his own experience.

Having received the record "that God hath given unto us eternal life," and that "he that hath the Son hath life," neither Satan nor man could persuade him that he had not received this record, or that he had any other trust than in Christ. Having seen—and he could not fail to see—the fruits of his faith in his own life, and having experienced "the joy of faith" in his own soul, he needed no other proofs, for this was the testimony of God's Spirit with his spirit that he was a child of God. Having thus obtained eternal life, and knowing that it was the gift of Him who makes no mistakes, and with whom—He being the same yesterday, to-day, and for ever—there is no variableness or the shadow of turning, he went on his way rejoicing, not looking to his sins, but to the everlasting covenant; not to himself, but to Jesus; not to his feelings and frames, or even his enjoyment of salvation, but resting on the fact that he was saved. To such, and to such only it is that God, speaking by the apostle, says, "Rejoice, and

again I say rejoice." Oh the unspeakable blessedness of
thus living and walking in Jesus—it is the very element of
holiness, the very beginning of heaven upon earth!

During the last twenty years of his life, Mr. Crabb
grew in grace, and it may be truly said that his last years
were his best. He was "in old age fat and flourishing,"
according to the promise, "to show that the Lord is
good." And thus it is with all those who exercise their
graces, it being equally true in spiritual as in earthly
things, "He that soweth sparingly, shall reap sparingly;
and he that soweth abundantly, shall reap abundantly."
He dug deep for spiritual gold, and dived deep for spiritual
pearls; and he neither dug nor dived in vain.

Let it not be supposed that in noticing these excellences
of Mr. Crabb, I desire to set him before the world as a
perfect character. To do this would be to dishonour him;
but more than this, to dishonour God. There was, however, in him what there is in most of the Lord's people,—
a degree of perfection, which is thus beautifully noticed
by Jeremy Taylor: "There is," he says, "a sort of God's
dear servants who walk in perfectness, who perfect holiness in the fear of God; and they have a degree of charity
and Divine knowledge more than we can estimate, and
more certain than the demonstrations of geometry, brighter
than the sun, and undeficient (unfailing) as the light of
heaven. This is to be felt, and not to be talked of; and
they who never touched it with their fingers may secretly,
perhaps, laugh at it in their hearts, and be never the wiser.
All that I shall now say of it is, that a good man is united
unto God as a flame touches a flame, and combines into
splendour and glory; so is the spirit of a man united unto
Christ by the Spirit of God. These are the friends of
God, and they best know God's mind; and they only that

are so, know how much such men do know,—they have a special unction from above." Mr. Crabb's perfection was in Jesus, and he desired to have no other completeness than in Him. Like other men, he had a body of sin and death to struggle with, in which he "groaned, being burdened." He was no stranger to the deceitfulness of his own heart, the conflicts between flesh and spirit, the hard struggle to maintain consistency, the depths of Satan, and the workings of self. He knew what it was to find his own wisdom to be folly, his own strength weakness, and what he imagined to be the work of the Spirit, to be often nothing more than the deceit of the flesh. Men judged of him, as they ever judge of one another, by what was external; but he judged himself by what he saw and knew to be within. Whilst they were commending him for his faithfulness, he was mourning over his want of it, whilst they were wondering at the grace vouchsafed to him, he was humbling himself in the dust before God, under deep views of indwelling corruption; and whilst they were extolling his diligence and zeal, he was weeping over his short comings and (as it appeared to him) his unprofitable life. Did God keep a registry of men's prayers, how affecting would be the record of the confessions, the self-loathings, the self-abasements, and self-condemnations of such a man as this before the Majesty of heaven! How truly is it said by Lockyer, that " A Christian's condition is made to speak Christ within and without,—in spirit, in flesh. The book is written within and without. In our souls, in our bodies we are made to bear the marks of the Lord Jesus,—marks broad and long, just like His in every circumstance. The plowers made long furrows on his back, as long as his life; he was acquainted with grief; — grief and he were of long acquaintance. His whole voyage about this lower world was in storms,—a man of sorrows,—his life made up of sighs, groans, tears, wounds, blood ; thus breathed, thus expired ; a mourning life, a bleeding death. And the servant is as his Lord—sufferers both as long as livers in this world."

CHAPTER XVII.

CONCLUDING REMARKS.

In concluding this brief Memoir, it may not be without profit to trace out some of the lessons which are to be learnt from the career of men who, like Mr. Crabb, "being dead yet speak."

We live in days in which flesh loves to glory; but the Lord sometimes pours contempt upon it, and takes to Himself the glory that belongs to Him; therefore it is that not only in the matter of conversion, but in the work of the ministry, we often find that He chooses "the foolish things of the world to confound the wise, the weak things of the world to confound the things which are mighty, and base things of the world, and things which are despised, to bring to nought those that are, that no flesh should glory in his presence."

In looking at what Mr. Crabb did, and endeavoured to do for his fellow men, we see that whilst many may labour and accomplish little, from the want of zeal and love, or because they are not sent of God, one poor, solitary, humble individual, without learning, without a name, and without station, by the power of the Holy Ghost, and sent by Him who alone can teach to profit, may do more "than they all."

We see further, that if one individual was enabled,

through grace, to accomplish what Mr. Crabb did, how much might be effected by the people of God were they to unite with one heart and one mind in the endeavour to save souls. With how little difficulty, by an united effort, might the Gospel be carried into every gipsy camp in England, and every gipsy child be brought under Christian instruction! To how many thousands of our countrymen, who now live in ignorance of their eternal destiny, and who, in the midst of civilization and intelligence, are sunk into a more demoralized condition than the people of heathen lands, might the Gospel be carried as a light to direct their feet into the ways of peace! How many who perish in our cities and towns, unpitied and unknown; and how many, who are trained in the dwellings around us for the service of Satan, might be plucked out of the hands of the destroyer! But, alas! there is no union. Men divide and dispute: one is of Paul, another of Apollos: one will support this "interest," and another that: what man bids or forbids receives attention; but when Christ bids His ministers preach the Gospel to every creature, the *command* is laid aside till those who bear the name of his ministers,—and many of whom arrogate to themselves the exclusive authority to promulgate His truth,—have settled how, and when, and where, and by whom and under what *earthly* direction perishing millions are to be saved from destruction.

> " Alas! our locks of strength are almost shorn ;
> Distracted counsels and divided aims
> Impede fair union ; and that mystic ROBE
> (That, all unrent, while on His gory cross
> The Martyr of Creation hung, remain'd,)
> Is torn to tatters underneath his throne
> By hands and hearts schismatically wild ! "

The success which was vouchsafed to the labours of Mr. Crabb may serve to show the hatefulness of sectarian bigotry and spiritual arrogance. The great Apostle rejoiced when Christ was preached, even though it was of contention; but many, alas! how many, of those who claim to be the successors of him and his fellow-labourers, and cry "Hear the church," despise, and would, if they could, silence the man who, in these "perilous times," would preach Christ in love to Him and love to souls! Alas! what is this but to forbid the life-boat to put off from the shore to the wrecked vessel, sinking with her numerous and perishing crew into the deep, because the mariners by whom it is manned, though ready to risk their lives to save their fellow-men, have not passed an examination before a Board of Navigation, or were not regularly brought up to the service. Such men dishonour Christ, and tacitly proclaim that those whom He honours He ought not to honour. Surely such men may well doubt, not merely whether they possess the spirit of Him who wept when He saw the hardness of men's hearts, but whether they have ever felt the value of their own souls. Oh! it is a solemn thing for men to act thus in days like these, when all that our martyrs suffered, and our patriots bled to secure for us and our children, is so little prized and so easily surrendered. This is no time—let carnal men cavil and dispute as they may—for division amongst those who love Jesus, and know the value of immortal souls; neither is it a time to look coldly on any that are Christ's, or to forbid them to preach the Gospel, whether it be in the house or in the street, on the quay or on shipboard, in established churches or dissenting chapels. If ever there was a time when it behoved the disciples of Jesus to rally round the standard of that truth which made us free, and can alone keep us and our children free, it is *now*, when its enemies are not only at the gates of our Zion, but have their adherents upon its ramparts and within its camp ;—when

> " Principle expires,
> And base expediency's polluted breath
> Falls like a mildew over minds and men ,"

—when England's church, the glory of our country as the sacred depository of the truth of God, the citadel of Protestantism, the faithful witness for Christ, totters to her base ;—when the fire on her altar burns faintly because of the rubbish which has been heaped upon it by un-hallowed hands ; and when the light of her candlestick grows dimmer and more dim. Oh ! what lessons are Popery and infidelity teaching the church of God ! and how solemnly are passing events speaking as with a voice from heaven !

> " Oh, that in light, from flames where Ridley died,
> Or Cranmer suffer'd in his burning death,
> The Church of England would her history read,
> And ponder, as she reads with eye of prayer,
> Till in that light her lethargy awake,
> And rising, like a giant from a sleep
> Enchanted, back the Romish chain would fall
> Dissever'd, from her limbs of glory dash'd
> In horror."

But the church listens not, hears not. Her voice is lifted up against the abominations of "the mother of harlots," against the sins of nations, the hypocrisy of individuals ; but she sees not her own crying sins, against which the God of truth has so long, "in divers manners," spoken from heaven, and against which He now makes bare his arm. Already the streaks of that day which is drawing nigh begin to gild the horizon, and make visible the shadows of things that are coming on the earth. Already the portentous sound of the approaching whirlwind which is to shake the church is heard in the distance; but those whose duty it is to watch, slumber and sleep "as do others," and cannot,—will not, —see or hear.

Ministers, in looking at one like Mr. Crabb, may see that where a man truly gives himself up to the service of God, he need be careful for nothing. The conviction of this saved him from many cares and many temptations. He lived by faith and not by sight, trusting in the faithfulness of God. We do not therefore find him moving from one sphere of labour to another to better his worldly circumstances, or advance the prosperity of his children. He was not afraid to trust all he had, and all events, present and future, to Him who was acquainted with his " downsitting and uprising;" put his tears 'into his bottle,' and took account of his very sighs; neither did he act upon the atheistical principle that a man can shorten his life in the service of Christ, as though God's promises that his people's strength should be equal to their day, and that " he who trusts in the Lord, mercy shall compass him about," were empty words. How often did the morning sun, when first on earth he " sheds his orient beams," visit his chamber and find him earlier still in earnest communion with Heaven! How long, how frequent, were his journeys through rain and tempest, frost and snow, to spread the knowledge of a Saviour's love! How often did the moon's radiant lamp light him on his "weary way," as, at the midnight hour he travelled from the sick man's room, and lengthened visits to the sons of woe! How often did he weep at the hardness of men's hearts, and struggle to bear con-

tumely and reproach, insult and injury for Him whose
support alone could bear him up! With a bad constitution he laboured without ceasing from his earliest
youth to the age of seventy-seven, or rather to a far
more advanced age; for he had that "length of days"
which made length of years, his hours of sleep having
seldom exceeded six. He knew that Christ has possession not only of the keys of hell, but of death, Rev. i. 18;
and that he should never enter his grave by chance, or
before his time, but when Christ Himself unlocked it.

We see, further, that those who serve God shall not
serve him in vain, and that in due time they shall reap, if
they faint not; that the Christian's path may be rugged,
but he shall be helped through every difficulty; that his
sorrows may be great, but they shall have an end; that
his conflicts may be severe, but he shall finally overcome;
that no enemy shall triumph over him, but in all things,
and under all circumstances, like James Crabb, he shall
be " more than conqueror through Him who loved him."

We discover, moreover, how God trains and disciplines His
people for future usefulness, and through what humbling
processes this is effected. " They will never," says Dyke,
" be fit for fighting, that have not been used to training ;
self-trial is training, and fiery-trial is fighting." Thus,
in the interval between Mr. Crabb's itinerancy and his
settling in Rumsey, he, in some measure, fell into a
worldly state, was deeply tried by adversity, and humbled
by spiritual declension. As the husbandman cuts the
too luxuriant shoots of the young germen close to the
ground, that in the appointed season it may burst forth
with fresh energy and vigour from the root, so the Lord
made him to pass through the same process, stopped him
in his rapid career, and laid all his fancied glory in the

dust, that he might be prepared for future usefulness and
come forth with renewed strength. "Thus," as Lockyer
says, "if God cast down, it is to raise up; if He humble,
it is to exalt; if He empty, it is to fill; if He kill, it is
to make alive; if He make sorrow long without, it is to
make joy strong within."

In Mr. Crabb the Christian has the picture of a man
downright in earnest;—no unimportant subject for our
contemplation in days like these. We see from his Diary,
that as a young man he set out on his Christian course
determined to know nothing but Christ, and with a resolution to take the kingdom of heaven by violence. He
commenced by turning his back broadly on the world
and setting his face Zionward. Having buckled on his
armour, he began at once the warfare against those no
mean enemies, Satan and the flesh; he searched out his
besetting sins, looked well to the citadel of his heart, and
took account of his very thoughts. It is impossible to
read the entries in his Diary, both when he was a youth
and when he was a preacher, set forth in former pages,
without being struck with the fixedness of his heart and
the inflexibility of his determination to serve and honour
God. His *desire* was to stand complete in all the will of
God; and God, who *hears* the desire of the humble, did
not leave him to desire in vain. His obedience was the
obedience of principle—the obedience of faith. His faith
rested on Christ, and from Him he drew all his motives
for the mortification of sin, for the performance of duty,
and for holiness of walk in the fear of God. All this was
kept alive by incessant wrestling with God, and this was
the mainspring that set all in motion. The value of looking at such a man's life is, that it leads us not only to see
that grace is a reality, but that the promises of God are

truly yea and amen in Christ Jesus. We see, further, that if we do ask, we *shall* have; if we do seek, we *shall* find; and if we do knock, it *shall* be opened to us: that whilst the grace of God makes a man holy, it makes him love to be so; that he who improves the talent he has, shall have more abundantly; and that if we seek *first* the kingdom of God and His righteousness, all other things *shall* be added to us. Moreover, as we see the glory of the sun in its bright coruscations on the waves of ocean, —in the light by which it makes visible the grandeur of created things,—in the colours with which it stoops to paint the tulip and the rose, and in its reflected radiance in the moon and stars, the rainbow, and the evening cloud,—so in the life of such a man we see and recognise in all its aspects, its developments, and its glory, the great truth, that God is LOVE. It stands out before us in bold relief,—in the very brightness of heaven; our hearts are warmed in its contemplation, — our affections are drawn out towards heaven, and our lips involuntarily burst forth from the fulness of the ravished heart,—GOD IS LOVE!

But, dear reader, it may be thou art too proud to stoop to learn of one who filled so lowly a place as Mr. Crabb did before God; but when thou lovest Jesus as he did, —when thou hast the deep concern for souls which he had—when thou labourest for the cause of thy God as he laboured, thou mayest well be forgiven this folly, if thou couldest be then guilty of it. As thou now art, thou hast need, though thou dost not feel it, to go to a meaner source for instruction—even to the ant—to learn of her to be more diligent; thou hast need to consider the inanimate creation itself, even the lilies of the field, that thou mayest see how God can show forth His glory in the meanest of His works, as well as in those which are the most magnificent; thou hast need to consider the heavens, the moon, and the stars, to learn to know thy nothingness and the greatness of Him by whom they were ordained.

But, reader, it may be thou art altogether a stranger to Jesus. If it be so, let the perusal of these pages lead thee to consider how thou standest with respect to eternity, and what thy everlasting destiny would be if thou wert now to be called to close thine eyes for ever upon time. Art thou like the foolish youth running to catch the bee, which as you follow flies, and which, couldest thou catch it, would but sting thee.* Oh, hasten not after that which, like the bee, eludes thy grasp, and which, if it were thine, would be but a golden nothing. Turn, turn to that blessed One now looking down upon thee, to win thee with His smile and draw thee by His Spirit. Dost thou not hear that touching voice, which now says to thee, "Come unto me and I will give thee rest." That voice is the voice of Him who died for sinners such as thou art— who, though rich, for thy sake became poor, that thou, through his poverty, mightest be made rich. It is He, even He who invites thee to accept at His hands, without money, and without price, pardon and peace, glory and eternal life. Oh! is thy heart made of adamant? Art thou wholly insensible to the voice of mercy, the beseechings of love? Wilt thou refuse to listen to Him? Shall He supplicate in vain? Can the world supply thy want of Christ? Can it save thy soul? Oh, stretch out thy hands, thy soul, to that willing, beseeching, waiting Saviour, lest thou be like one who, dying in thy state, stretched out his hands to them that stood by, and cried in vain, *"Call time! oh, call time again!"* It may be

* Sequendo labitur, assequendo læditur.

thou hast regarded religion as a despoiler, who would rob thee of thy pleasures and give thee nothing in return ; but be not deceived, she will take from thee nothing but thy sin and misery. She will not despoil thee of thy riches, nor thine honours, nor thy rank, if thou hast them ; but gild them with grace and glory, so that they shall help thee forward heavenwards. Possessing Jesus, those things to which thou now clingest will lose their charm, and that which thou now prizest will be accounted to be what it is in truth,—vanity. Thy present hopes will be discovered to be delusions, and thy present trust, destruction. But fear not, thou wilt not suffer loss, for if Christ be thine, all things will be thine ; thou shalt drink of the rivers of pleasure flowing from beneath the throne of God ; thou shalt dwell in that light which is sown to the righteous, and taste of that joy which is the portion of the upright ; thou shalt have a hope blooming with immortality, and a trust based on omnipotence itself. Oh, then,

> " Seek that thou may'st find, and
> God will give thee His new name, and write it on thy heart :
> A name better than of sons, a name dearer than of daughters,
> A name of union, peace, and praise."

To that God—at whose footstool I lay this feeble effort to speak of His doings and proclaim His faithfulness and truth—be glory for ever.

LONDON :
PRINTED BY WILLIAM TYLER,
BOLT-COURT.

ČPSIA information can be obtained at www.ICGtesting.com
Printed in the USA
LVOW10s1951141113

361326LV00022B/828/P

9 781115 326490